NOTES ON BUDDHIST LAW

BY THE JUDICIAL COMMISSIONER, BRITISH BURMA

III.—MARRIAGE. Jardine, Sir John

PREFACE

(Including Introductory Remarks by Dr. E. Forchammer, Professor of Pali)

1. Translation of the Wonnana Dhammathat on Marriage : with a Commentary.

2. Translation of the Wonnana Dhammathat on Divorce : with a Commentary.

APPENDICES

A. Translation of the Wini Tsaya Paka Thani Dhammathat on Marriage and Divorce.

B. Cases illustrative of the Buddhist Law as now administered in the Court of the Judicial Commissioner of British Burma and the Subordinate Courts.

RANGOON : OFFICE OF THE SUPDT. GOVT. PRINTING AND STATY., BURMA. NOVEMBER 1953.

Price,—2·25]

take a fourth share amongst them, others that the eldest son takes this fourth, while Moung Tet Too is clear that the mother keeps all until her death. One Native Judge of long experience had never had such a case before him : another had, but only once. A third venerable Judge, on being consulted as to the meaning of texts, compared himself to a man wakening in a dream of times gone-by. Several who insist that by strict law a man may divorce his wife, or a wife her husband without any cause whatever, have stated that they never themselves had occasion to pass any such decree. All the many Native Judges whom I have consulted, whether they held that opinion or not, are united in saying that where one party absolutely objects to a divorce and refuses to ratify or acquiesce in an abandonment, the only possible way of effecting a divorce is by suit and decree in a Civil Court. But some have stated the rule at first as if the fiat of the divorcing party were sufficient, and then have limited their meaning and stated that such fiat of the party or award of elderly persons had no efficacy in itself. The difference of statement is something like what foreigners might make about the English law, in asserting from observation of the fact that many injured wives suffered desertion and adultery without complaint, that the English law empowered the husband to commit such wrongs, or from knowing the effect, not the cause of judicial separation, that he has a right to injure her provided he satisfies his wife with a separate establishment. These confusions result partly from the vagueness of the *Menu Kyay* and the universal ignorance of the Hindu codes, but chiefly from the prevalent practice of compromise.

2. It is plain that some rules of interpretation are required in construing old books of Burmese law, especially as we have no reports of judicial decisions. The Dhammathats show very clearly that the writers were avowedly and strongly influenced by notions, however derived, of what was reasonable and equitable. I would therefore suggest that some of our own rules of interpretation may fairly be applied, such as " the established rule of construction that " general words and phrases, however wide and compre- " hensive in their literal sense, must be construed as bearing " only on the immediate object of the Act, and as not " altering the general policy of the law, unless, of course, " no reasonable sense can be applied to them consistently " with the intention of preserving that policy untouched " (Maxwell on Statutes, Chapter 3). Injustice and absurdity, the impairing of obligations and allowing advantage to the

wrong-doer, must also be avoided. The reasons given in the Dhammathats for the rules propounded, some of which look like judicial decisions, confirm this view. A foreigner reading the statute mentioned by Lord Hale, which, imposed fines "at the King's pleasure," would infer that the King of England might impose fines at his mere caprice. But on consulting a lawyer he would be told that the King is bound by the interpretation of the Judges, who have ruled that the phrase really means that the King's power was to be exercised in his Courts and by his Justices. Another principle of criticism is that the real meaning of the Burmese must be ascertained by reference to the Pali Text, which again may require elucidation from the Sanskrit originals of Hindu law.

3. The *Menu Kyay* appears to me fuller than most of the Dhammathats. But in the present dearth of learning, it is as difficult to appraise its authority as to determine its age or the name of the author. Moung Tet Too, after instituting inquiries at Mandalay, discovered no clue to these secrets. Dr. Richardson mentions none. No Pali edition is known, and it is probably a compilation made from other Dhammathats. Several Burman Judges have spoken to me of the *Manoo Wonnana*, the *Manoo Thara Shwe Myeen*, and the *Manoo Thaya Paka Thani* as being authorities superior to the *Menu Kyay*. It is certain that the elucidation of the last will be aided by a study of the others; and as I am supplying copies of the *Wonnana* to every Court in the province, I have devoted some time from my judicial duties to the translation into English of parts of Moung Tet Too's edition. It is stated by Colonel Browne to have been compiled from older editions by the learned nobleman Wonna Dhamma Kyaw Deng in A.D. 1772, the same who in 1770 had finished the *Shwe Myeen*. He was Prime Minister at Ava in the reign of King Tsheng-bhoo-sheng, a son of the great Alompra.

4. The *Wonnana* in Moung Tet Too's edition gives a clearer and more compendious view of the law of marriage than the *Menu Kyay* affords. In the latter we must refer to portions of Books 5, 6, and 12: in this *Wonnana* the scattered provisions have been placed in two chapters, one on marriage, the other on divorce, and these are the chapters I now present to the English Judges. In my commentaries I draw attention to the corresponding parts of the *Menu Kyay* and to judicial decisions. In obscure passages I have here and there referred to the *Shwe Myeen* or got Dr. Forchhammer to examine the palm-leaf

manuscript of the *Wagaru* in his possession. Words used to help the sense are italicised or placed in parentheses The translations were made by my interpreter, Mr. Minus, who was aided by Moung San, a Burman clerk. The sense was ascertained in consultation with ancient Judges like Oo Wike, the well known Htee Taga of Pegu, and Moung Htine of Prome; and the English of the more important parts has been revised by myself, with an endeavour to follow the Burmese closely while making the meaning apparent; and in many instances citing the parallel Hindu text. But some knowledge of Burmese is almost essential to a fair understanding of the meaning, and I presume that the reader knows something of that language.

5. The reader will, I believe, be struck with the precision of the Minister Kyaw Deng. The cases are stated with abrupt clearness; some seem to have been actual suits; and the reasons of decision often given, elsewhere plainly implied, are similar to those that govern our own Courts. A man must not get advantage from his own fraud. A minor must get relief against surprise or mistake. A voidable marriage shall not be annulled after consummation except for good reasons. A husband is bound to look after his own honour. The wrongs entitling to divorce are specifically stated, while the minor causes of quarrel between married couples are carefully distinguished as matters to be settled in the domestic forum by tact, good temper, and submission to a plain conjugal morality based on religious sanctions. Like the other Dhammathats, this one sets forth with brevity but clearness the moral obligations which are implied in the lawful union of the sexes. This fact is brought out the more clearly when we compare the compendious statements of the *Wonnana* with the ampler descriptions and longer arguments of the *Menu Kyay* The best way of studying the *Menu Kyay* seems to be by treating the *Wonnana* as a guide. At the same time I have quoted at length some fervent applications of the solemnest dogmas of Buddhism to married life. Even were they not imbedded in the law, they would be relevant to the present subject. We all admit that the maxims of St. Paul, "Husbands, love your wives, wives, obey your husbands," do in countless ways affect the millions of Christendom who are governed by laws of which Christianity is one of the bases; and it seems to me a wrong principle of criticism to assume that any civilized nation governed by such jurists as Kyaw Deng would be guided in matters of the sexes by the dry dictates of artificial laws.

or by mere theological **dogmas** and not by an established morality to which civil laws are merely ancillary. This is a point I would press upon foreign Judges ; and I deeply regret my own incapacity to state the literature by which I suspect many of the allusions should be explained, and from which, perhaps, the finished literary portraits of the seven kinds of wives and the solemn religious injunctions of the *Menu Kyay* are taken in whole or part. Without a considerable knowledge of the ancient ideas of a people, foreigners are apt to make mistakes about their family customs : any estimate of the English, for instance, would be bad without a knowledge of the Bible : to understand the Dhammathats, we must refer to the Hindu *Manu* and the Buddhist sacred canon. The Courts of the country, too, have ample means of getting at decisions passed by Burman Judges : some of these, collected at random on my last inspection tour, I have printed in an appendix, as also a translation of the chapters on marriage and divorce in the *Wini Tsaya Paka Thani* Dhammathat. I would fain express a hope that the art of translating law-books, lost apparently for the last 35 years, will be followed by others having more time at their disposal and a better acquaintance with the language, the literature, and the custom. Men with these attainments will some day perhaps find out why the *Wonnana* affirms more completely than the *Menu Kyay* the control of parents over the betrothals of children, and why the latter contains the procedure by eloping three times, incidents on which, with other things, the *Wagaru* and the *Wonnana* are silent. Competent scholars ought without difficulty to ascertain the relative ages of the Dhammathats, and the reason why Books 5 and 12 of the *Menu Kyay* contain with variations much of the same matter. It is likely enough that different rules were propounded to suit the changing times or the peculiar circumstances of different parts of the country : as among ourselves a lately acquired province or a region of wild tribes is treated differently to the older territories. We need not be surprised at finding several schools of law or rules diverging under the influence of religion or philosophy as in India and Rome We know well enough the effect of conquest on the old law by long experience in the Indian Empire and from both English and Roman history. But since Dr. Richardson's days a generation has passed away without leaving much deposit of learning and research, and we are in a worse position for understanding the effect of Alompra's conquest of the Talaings. If, however, we can get the manuscript of the *Wagaru* Dhammathat translated and edited, we may even now be able to find out something : and in such inquiries the account of the customs of the Chin tribe, compiled by the Sitkeh of Myaydeh, Moung Tet Byu, might be useful. To stimulate inquiry, I have offered a prize of Rs. 1,000, to be adjudged by my colleagues in the Educational Syndicate of British Burma, for the best essay explanatory of the rise and progress of the Buddhist law. The time has come for a change like the Revival of Letters: once a general interest is awakened light will pour in from different directions, and some day we may have translations from the Pali editions, without which the Burmese Dhammathats will never be rightly understood. I am convinced that the Pali scholar ought to have preceded the Judge.* Pretending to no such learning, I have printed the chapters on marriage and divorce with a view to aid the Courts of this province to understand the general ideas of the Burmese, and the influence of the Hindu law on Turanian customs. Those who have sneered at them as barbarous will, I believe, be astonished at the excellence of the rules and the soundness of the reasons cited in the texts. I add that these subjects are not antiquarian, but are matter for all the Courts, as even the most youthful Myo-oke has a matrimonial jurisdiction which, if unregulated by defined principles, might unsettle the whole frame of society. They are not yet defined. Just as a judgment of my own on inheritance displays the unsettled state of that part of Buddhist law at present, so do the doubts entertained by Quinton J. on the question of *ex-parte* divorce become very apparent in his judgments appended. It is clear that he waited for authorities before declaring the law, and as Mr. Sandford promoted the copying of the palm-leaf and the printing of the copies, so I continue the work by offering a translation to my colleagues in the administration of justice.

RANGOON :   }   **JOHN JARDINE,**

The 12th December 1882.   *Judicial Commissioner.*

---

* Since writing this Preface I have submitted the proofs of the translations to Dr. E. Forchhammer, the learned Professor of Pali. I have embodied his corrections and explanations in the form of remarks, which I am persuaded will be as interesting to ordinary Burmans as acceptable to European scholars. They explain some of the connections between the Burman and Indian laws, the allusions to earlier literature, the meaning of the Pali originals of the Burmese texts, and the force of the words used to denote abandonment, separation, and divorce. This learning has hitherto been beyond the reach of the Judges, whether European or Burmese. Dr. Forchhammer's Introductory remarks are I believe the first attempt at a historical account of the development of the law of Burma.

Introductory Remarks by Dr. E. Forchhammer, Professor of Pali.

THE *caltari ariyasaccani*, or "the four great truths," are the four theses upon which the whole doctrine of Buddha is based ; they are, briefly expressed, *dukkham, samudayo nirodho*, and *maggo*, or "suffering, the cause of suffering, the cessation of suffering, the path leading to the cessation of suffering."

The existence of every sentient being, the aggregate of form, sensation, perception, discrimination, conscio usness, is one of misery. Existence is the necessary result of an antecedent cause : "from error springs karma, from karma "springs consciousness, from consciousness springs the "organized being, from the organized being springs the six "organs of sense, from the six organs of sense springs "contact, from contact springs sensation, from sensation "springs desire, from desire springs attachment, from "attachment springs birth, from birth springs decay and "death, sorrow, lamentation, pain, grief, and despair." Existence therefore is the result of ignorance of the truth, and especially of the "four great truths." By human desire (*tanha*) continued existence is produced ; cessation of suffering (*i.e.*, existence) is effected by the destruction of the five khandas (form, sensation, perception, discrimination, con-sciousness) and the exercise of the eight angas— "right views, right thoughts, right speech, right actions, "right living, right exertion, right recollection, right "meditation," by which the extinction of human passion may be obtained. Destruction of human passion leads to the "four paths," or "four stages of sanctification "leading to Nirvana, and without which Nirvana cannot be "attained."

According to Manu, marriage is one of the ten sacra- ments necessary for regeneration of men of the twice-born classes, and the only sacrament for women and sudras ; one must have a son to save him from a place of torment called "put," and marriage, as the primary means to that end, becomes a religious necessity. If a Brahman have not read the Veda, if he have not begotten a son, and if he have not performed sacrifices, yet shall aim at final beautitude, he shall sink to a place of degradation.

The founder of Buddhism regards birth as the result of desire and attachment, arising from *error* and ending in *misery*. To suppress desire, lust, he enjoins upon all sentient beings ; their progress towards Nirvana is thereby hastened and the pain of birth and misery of existence spared to others. "Abandon the different kinds of desire (founded "on) child, wife, father, mother, wealth, corn, relations, and "wander lonely like the rhinoceros. Let a wise man, "having discovered that such is attachment, that there is "in it but little happiness, that it is but insipid, that it is "mere affection, that it is a fish-hook, walk alone like a "rhinoceros."—(*Khaggavisana Sutta*.)

"He who has children grieves on account of the child- "ren ; he who has cattle, grieves likewise on account of the "cattle ; he who has no objects of desire, does not indeed "grieve ; thus said Bhagava (Budda)."—*Dania Sutta*, 17.

A wise man should avoid married life as it it were a burning pit of live coals."—*Dhammika Sutta*.

"If any one avoids the pleasures of the senses as (one would) "crush the head of a snake with the foot, that wise "man overcomes the dart of sorrow in this world."— *Rama Sutta*, 3.

Whether we look at the private life of Gautama, or at his system of ethics or philosophy, or at the tenour of his discourses to the laity, we fail to discover traits which would allow the inference of Gautama intending to justify marriage as a sacrament or as a status. Compelled to recognise the then existing condition of society, he pronounces a goodwife a blessing (mangala sutta), inveighs against adultery, but persistently discourages the state of "householder" and the contracting of family attachments of any kind. He has framed no laws for the state of marriage. *Buddhist law* exists only for the *Buddhist priesth od* and does not affect any other social status ; the rules and regulations contained in the *Vinayapitakam*, or Code of Monastic Discipline, tend towards a rigid social disconnection and emanciption from secular legislation and influence. In his lay-discourses he raises the woman to a higher position by according her, provided she has aban- doned this world of desire and passion, the right to enter the "paths" which excludes marriage or the enjoyment of sexual intercourse. Gautama did not elevate the position of the *wife*, but that of the *woman*, by enfranchising her from the perpetual tutelage to which she was condemned by the Hindu law, and by placing her destiny in her own hands, dependent on her own individual exertion and power to balance her merit and demerit against the reckoning in the next existence.

Strictly speaking, there is *no* Buddhist law of marriage. Gautama treats of the duties, of the grounds and obligations, of laymen from a general and ethic point of view. Marriage law and marriage customs, prevalent among the various nations and tribes who have embraced Buddhism, have not materially altered through its introduction; they are indigenous and peculiar to the Buddhists, Tartars, Thibetans, Laos, Burmese, and Sinhalese. With some nations the introduction of Buddhism has effected unimportant changes, such as the discontinuance of the slaughter of animals at the wedding.

The positive laws contained in the Burmese law books regulating marriage, divorce, separation, abandonment, and division of property can nearly all be traced to the earliest law books of Hinduic India. Burmese law appears not to have been influenced by the more modern schools of Benares, Mithila, Bengal, Dravida, and Maharashtra; it has a development and history of its own, but is based upon the ancient codes of Manu and Yajnavalkya.

Whatever notions the Burmans may have as to the antiquity of their Dhammathats, which they ascribe to Manu, investigations into the history of the Burmans and their literature leave but little doubt that the Burmese tongue was not reduced to writing prior to Anawratha's conquest (10th century A.D.) of the Talaing dominions, and that they possessed no written books in their own idiom before this event took place.

Buddhism had no connected history and no firm footing in Burma till Anawratha and his successors, in conjunction with the Talaing kings of the 14th and 15th centuries, exerted their power in behalf of Buddhism and helped it to a decided and lasting predominance over Brahmanism. Burmese and Talaing histories mention the great learning in the Vedas, astronomy, and medicine of several kings of the early dynasties ruling in Prome and Pugan; but from these remote periods no other literary testimonies have come down to us than a few inscriptions in Sanskrit written with Nagari (and not with Burmese) characters and a number of Sanskrit derivations, chiefly astronomical terms, in the Burmese idiom. As Hindu colonies are known to have clustered at very remote periods round the capitals of Burmese kings, and as Brahmans always possessed a great influence at Burmese Courts, the possibility need not be excluded of Hindu Dhammathats having been known or even compiled at the Courts of ancient Kings of Prome and perhaps also Pugan. If this has been the case, they must have been composed in Sanskrit for the use of the

Court only ; but as no trace of such work has as yet been discovered, the age of the Burmese law-literature falls within the last eight hundred years, beginning with the establishment of Buddhism at Pugan in the 11th century, the reducing of the Burmese idiom by means of the Talaing alphabet, and the translation into Burmese of the holy scriptures, and probably also law-book, from "the five elephant loads of Talaing literature," which Anawratha took from Thatone, the capital of the conquered Muns. In the 15th century a brisk intercourse arose between the Burmese and Sinhalese religious communities ; the Buddhist literature of the sacred island superseded the Talaing-Pali literature, "and the national vanity of the Burmans of course prevents "them from acknowledging their indebtedness to the "conquered race, the Talaings." The Sinhalese, however, possess no law-books corresponding to the Burmese Dhammathats, and we must therefore, in the first instance, look to the Talaings to obtain a clue as to the origin of the Burmese law-books in the form we at present possess them.

The authenticated history of the Talaings begins with the 13th century before Christ, when Sona and Uttara, two Buddhist missionaries, landed at Golanagara, a settlement of the Gangetic Gandas (the Gaurs) on the shores of Suvannabhummi, which comprised the coast from the Sittoung river to the Strait. The oldest Talaing inscriptions date back to the 4th century A.D., and the lythic characters are almost identical with the Dravidian-Vengi alphabet of the same period. In the 5th century A.D., Budhaghosha, the great commentator of the Buddhist holy scriptures, brought complete copies of the *Pitakat* and the commentaries, and also Hindu law books, from Ceylon and India to Ramañña, the country of the Talaings. In the 8th and 9th centuries Buddhism was almost suppressed by the Kings of Pegu, who were zealous Brahmans. In the 10th and 11th centuries the Burmans conquered the Talaing dominions ; in the 13th, 14th, and 15th centuries the Muns again gained independence, and Buddhism and Talaing literature revived. At the close of the 15th and the beginning of the 16th centuries a Talaing hero, Budhaghosha, acquired great fame as a jurist ; he was called to the Courts of Pugan and the King of Siam to settle difficult law disputes. With him begins the authenticated history of Burmese Dhamma-thats. I have found a copy of the probably most ancient version of the *Manoo Sara* extant ; Budhaghosha translated it as he himself expressly states, from the original Talaing into Pali and Burmese : "I, the hero Budhaghosha,

" desirous of promoting the interest of religion, translated
" faithfully (according to the letter) the *Vagaru* Dhammathat
"written in the Talaing language." The Talaing version, he
further states, was arranged by Wagaru (Wah-ra-roo), a King
of Martaban, who began his reign in the year 1280 A.D.

As the text of the present versions of the *Manoo Sara
Shwe Myeen* and the *Manoo Wonnina* are based upon the
text of the *Wagaru*, we can for the present dispense with
the two mythical recensions of the *Manoo Sara*, which are
asserted by the Burmans to have been composed at very
remote periods by Manusara and Pyoc-meng-tee, the third
King of the Pugan dynasty, who is said to have reigned
about 168 A.D. The *Wagaru* is certainly based on the
codes of Manu and Yajnavalkya, and I do not hesitate to
assert that Hindu law was first appropriated by the Talaings
and accommodated to their social status and religion. The
pretensions of the Burmans to the possession of original or
more ancient recensions of the *Manoo Sara* than the
Wagaru is not borne out by their history or the history of
their literature.

The Pali-Burmese versions of the *Man o Sara*, the
Manoo Sara Shwe Myeen, the *Wonnana*, the *Dhamma'hat
Kwon Kya*, the *Wini Tsaya Paka Thani*, and the *Menu
Kyay* have been prepared under the successor of Alompra ;
Zin-pyoo-mya-shin greatly encouraged the revival of
literature : it was also he who caused about 250 Sanskrit
works to be translated into Burmese.

From a passage in the *Manoo Wonn na* (Vol. 1, s. 157) it
would appear that the compiler consulted the *Manoo Reng* ;
he says : ' In some olden scriptures, the 'sapuma' occurring
in the gatha under comment is wrongly translated by
paramour." Of all Dhammathats which I have consulted,
it is only the *Manoo Reng* which translates the passage
erroneously with " paramour." The *Manoo Reng* appears
to me to have been the first and certainly not very scholarly
attempt to reduce the prose text of the *Wagaru* to verses ;
neither the Burmese nor Pali exhibit any traces of high age
which would justify us to relegate the age of the *Manoo Reng*
to a more distant period than the 17th century. The
reunion we now possess in a printed edition is older than
the *Wonnana, Manoo Thara Shwe Myeen*, and the *My en
Kyay*, for the following two reasons :—(1) The Talaing
Dhammathats contain the subject matter divided into the
traditional 18 chapters ; they contain no admixture from
Buddhist "hpiathtoons" and Zats, nor digressions on
Buddhist ethics, nor extracts from the *Pitakas* or

Budhaghosha's commentaries; they appear to be the uncontaminated outgrowth, altered somewhat and adapted to the social status of the Talaings, of the original codes of Manu. The first 18 pages of the *Manoo Reng* have evidently been added from a Burmese hpiathtoon, or "decisions," a branch of Burmese law-literature extracted from the *Jatakas*, especially the *Mahosadha* and *Vidhura-jataka*, in which Bodhisat (the future Buddha) appears in the capacity of a wise judge. His decisions have been compiled into a sort of code of precedents; they have preceded the use of Manu's Dhammathats amongst the Burmans. The *Dvattatoung hpiathtoon*, the *Adasamukha, Zalakadewi, Zalimeng, Upali, Kakawonnanameng hpiathtoons* are all Buddhistic and form the most ancient portion of the Burmese law-literature. The rest however of the *Manoo Reng* follows closely the oldest recension of the *Manoo Sara* of the 15th century, and does not contain the numerous additions to both the Pali and Burmese texts which we find in the *Wonnana Shwe Myeen* and *Menu Kyay*. We can safely put the age of the *Manoo Reng* at about 200 years. (2) The *Wonnana* adduces and corrects certain readings which occur, as far as known, only in the *Manoo Reng*. The law-books compiled at the close of the last century may be considered as a compromise between the Burmese hpiathtoons and the Manus as inherited from the Talaings; the great bulk of the Talaing literature was destroyed by Alompra. The *Menu Kyay* contains, dispersed between specifically *Manuic* enactments, extracts from the *milinda Panha*, from the *Mahosadha* and *Vidhurajatakas*, from Budhaghosha's *Visuddhimaggo* and the *Samaniapsadika*, the same author's commentary on the *Vinyapitakam* (the Buddhist Code of Monastic Discipline); it is also a significant fact that Buddhist priests had to some extent lost their prerogative of being alone responsible to the sanigha, or the assembled priesthood, and of being exempted from the ruling and laws of secular authorities. Zin-pyoo-mya-shin suppressed by stringent measures the eternal quarelling of the Punnas (Brahmans) and ponegyees at his Court, and in case of criminal transgressions on part of members of the Buddhist priesthood, assumed the power of punishing crime according to the rules of Parajikan, that is, he declared them excluded from the priesthood, punished them as he would ordinary laymen, and had the laws regulating the conduct of priests incorporated in the secular law books. From the *Suttapitakam* the author of the *Menu Kyay* extract the discourse of Yasodhara, the wife of Gautama, before he became Buddha, on the "seven kinds of wives," and in two places (page 343 and 357) he gives legal importance to the Kammavipako, *i.e.*, the theory of good and bad results of good and evil deeds. Kammavipako is a technical term in Buddhist ethics, with a definite and well-ascertainable meaning, which admits of no empiric interpretation. The theory is fully explained in the *cula Kammu Bhauga Sutta* or *Subha Sutta*, which is well known and popular amongst the Burmans. I insert a full translation of the Sutta. (See Supplement, *Subha Sutta*). A man marries a girl whose parents are not afflicted with any hereditary disease, such as leprosy, madness, cancer, syphilis, &c., which in the *Wagaru* are collectively called "hinaroga," or wasting diseases, and permit, according to Manu, supersession of, and according to the *Menu Kyay*, separation from, the diseased wife. The girl, on account of bad deeds in a former existence, is doomed to be attacked, after her marriage, by leprosy, or, after giving birth to a child, by madness or cancer, her husband is aware of the cause of the disease ; he may himself succumb to it, his offspring will inherit it ; and the law allows in such cases separation or supersession. An instructive illustration of the Kammavipako occurs in the *Mahanarada-Jataka* : —" The "(girl) Rucha then related what had occurred to her in former "births and the reason why she was now only a woman. "Fourteen births previously she was a nobleman, but an "adulterer. In the next birth she was again a noble through ' the power of previous merit and gave much alms ; but "when she died she had to leave the merit thus acquired "like a mine of wealth hidden in the ground, and for her " previous demerit she was born in the Rowra hell, where " she remained 2880 koti of years. She was next born as a " vigorous ram in the country called Bhennuka ; again she " was a monkey and a draught-bullock, then born among sava- " ges, and was neither a male nor a female. After this she "was the dewi of the Sakra King, then the wife of a libertine, " and last of all the daughter of the King of Mithila."

According to Manu and the Vishnu Smriti, leprosy is the result of crimes of the highest degree ; an incendiary will be punished with madness. (Compare the *Subha Sutta* with the chapters on Transmigration in the *Institutes of Vishnu* Sacred Books of the East, Vol. VII.)

The *Manoo Wonnana* and *Menu Kyay* contain also numerous extracts from the *Samudrika lakshanam* and *Iti* (stri) *sastra*, especially when treating of the physical qualities of women and the different kinds of virgins. The *Wonnana* refers in the Burmese text (not in the Pali) frequently to a set of books beginning with the *Vyakaranas*. Zin-pyco-mya-shin, the successor of Alompra, had, as already stated, a number of Sanskrit works translated into Burmese, and the list of books begins with *Vopadeva's Sanskrit Grammar*, and contains besides works on astrology, palmistry, medicine, and erotics.

The Burmese have in past centuries been zealous Buddhists, their ways of life, their social and private institution, are thoroughly Buddhistic. The Burmese nat-worship is generally considered as a remains of aboriginal demonology, but it is different in kind from that of non-Buddhistic but cognate tribes, such as the Khyins. The Burmese fairies and sprites of trees and lakes, the tutelary nats of cities, houses, and boats, the nagas and ogres, and the mode of propitiating them, are reflections of the devas and prakshas occurring so frequently in the Buddhist *jatakas* and other portions of the *Suttapitakam*. Very few of Burmese notions, customs, and habits can with any degree of certainty be called *native* taken in the sense of aboriginal and non-Buddhistic : the Burmans themselves would repudiate the idea of having still the tatters of their former savage condition clinging to them. Although there be no " Buddhist law of marriage," yet there is no justification in looking upon Burmese marriage in any other light than that of Buddhist ethics ; not so much as they are expounded by the severe ascetic Buddha, the " exterminator," as he was justly called by his adversaries, but as they were interpreted, a thousand years after Gautama, in the commentaries of Budhaghosha and Dhammapala, who took cognisance of the existing state of society and provided a practical code of moral discipline for the Buddhist laymen, whose status as " householders " had been so little recognised by the founder of Buddhism.

Gautama excluded marriage from the " eight stage of a man's life ;" in the " five silas," which are binding on all Buddhists, sexual intercourse is prohibited ; but in the commentaries, the *Abrahmacariya*, when relating to laymen, is defined as adultery, fornication, and other inordinate sexual practices. As already stated, the commentary to the five Vinaya books, the commentaries to the *Suttapitakam*, the *Visuddhimmaggo*, and portions of the *Jatakas*, contribute largely to the contents of the *Wonana Manoo Kyay* and other modern law-books.

The Talaing written idiom contains a considerable number of Pali derivatives which are technical law terms. The Pali words have been so altered that we can justly infer that they had become part and parcel of the Talaing at a remote period, and that Dhammathats have long been in use. The Burmese literary language, which often contains 50 per cent of Pali derivatives, has incorporated hardly any technical terms peculiar to the Menu Dhammathats, and has not yet begun the process of Burmanizing them This appears to point to a but recent introduction and general use of the Dhammathats, which in this century gradually usurped the place of the Buddhistic "hpiathoons." In Burmese "histories of literature" mention is rarely made of Dhammathats prior to the close of the last century, from which we may infer that though Dhammathats may have existed, they were but little known.

[SUPPLEMENT]

Subha Sutta (as translated by Rev. Mr. Gogerly in Ceylon British Royal Asiatic Society Journal, 1846).

WHEN Bagawa was residing near Sewat, in the monastery founded by Anātha Pindiko at Jetawany, a young man named Subha, the son of Yodeyya came to his residence and, after a respectful salutation, sat down. Being seated he said, "Venerable Gautama, from what cause or by what "means is it that among mankind some persons are in pros- "perous and others in adverse circumstances ? It is seen, "Venerable Gautama, that some men are short lived, while "others live long ; some are much diseased, while others "have good health ; some are disgusting in appearance, while "others are beautiful ; some are without influence, while "others are powerful ; some are poor, while others are rich ; "some are ignoble, while others are high-born ; some are "wise, while others are foolish ; from what cause, Venerable "Gautama, or by what means is it that among mankind "some are prosperous while others are in adversity ?"

"Young man, living beings receive the results of their own conduct : their conduct forms their inheritance, their birth, their relationship, their circumstances in life ; conduct apportions to living beings prosperity or adversity."

"I do not distinctly understand that which has been thus briefly and obscurely spoken by the Venerable Gautama ; will the Venerable Gautama be pleased to explain fully the doctrine which has been thus briefly stated so that I may comprehend it ?"

"If this be your wish young man, attend carefully and I will explain it." Subha, the son of Yodeyya, replied," Let

"the Venerable one do so ;" upon which Bagawa said,—
" If in this world a woman or a man be a destroyer of life,
" cruel, bloody-handed, ever-slaughtering, and destitute of
" kindness towards living being, upon the dissolution of his
" frame by death, in consequence of the conduct to which
" he has thus been so fully accustomed, he will be born in
" hell, wretched, miserable, and tormented ; but if upon the
" dissolution of his frame by death he be not born in hell,
" wretched, miserable, and tormented, but again becomes a
" man, wherever he may be born he will be short lived.
" The path which leads to shortness of life is this : the being
" a destroyer of life, cruel, bloody-handed, ever-slaughtering,
" and destitute of kindness towards every living thing.

" If in this world a woman or a man abstain from
" destroying life, lay aside the club and the knife ; if he be
" gentle and compassionate to all living being, upon the
" dissolution of his frame by death, in consequence of the
" conduct to which he has been so fully accustomed, he
" will be born in heaven in a state of happiness, or if he be
" not born in heaven but again becomes a man, wherever
" he may be born he will be long lived. The path which
" leads to longevity is this : the abstaining from destroying
" life, the laying aside the club and the knife, and the
" being gentle and compassionate to every living thing.

" If in this world a woman or a man be a tormentor of
" living beings with the hand, with stones, sticks, or knives,
" upon the dissolution of his frame by death, in conse-
" quence of the conduct to which he has thus been so fully
" accustomed, he will be born in hell, wretched, miserable,
" and tormented ; but if upon the dissolution of his frame by
" death he be not born in hell, but if he again become a
" man, wherever he may be born he will be much afflicted
" with disease. The path which leads to a state of disease
" is this : to be a tormentor of living beings with the hand,
" with stones, with sticks, or with knives.

If in this world a woman or a man be not a tormentor of
" living beings with the hand, with stones, with sticks, or with
" knives, upon the dissolution of his frame by death, in
" consequence of the conduct to which he has been so fully
" accustomed, he will be born in heaven in a state of happi-
" ness ; or if he be not born in heaven, but if he again become
" a man, wherever he may be born he will enjoy good health.
" The path which leads to the enjoyment of good health is
" this : to abstain from tormenting living beings with the hand,
" with stones, with sticks, or with knives.

" In this world a woman or a man is wrathful and very
" passionate ; if when a few words are spoken he becomes
" angry, wrathful, enraged, and malicious, giving way to
" anger, hatred, and discontent, upon the dissolution of his
" frame by death, in consequence of the conduct to which he
" has been so fully accustomed he will be born in hell,
" wretched, miserable, and tormented, or if he be not born in
" hell, but if he again become a man, wherever he may be born
" he will be ill-favoured.   The path which leads to ugliness is
" this : to be wrathful and passionate when a few words are
" spoken, to be angry. wrathful, enraged, and malicious,
" giving way to anger, hatred, and discontent.

" In this world a woman or a man is neither wrathful nor
" passionate, but when much provocation is given is not angry,
" wrathful, enraged, nor malicious, and does not give way to
" anger, hatred, or discontent ; he, in consequence of the con-
" duct to which he has been so fully accustomed, upon the
" dissolution of his frame by death will be born in heaven in a
" state of happiness ; or if he be not born in heaven, but if he
" again become a man, wherever he may be born he will be
" beautiful.   The path for obtaining personal beauty is to be
" free from anger and passion ; even when much provocation is
" given to be neither angry, wrathful, enraged, nor malicious,
" and to avoid giving way to anger, hatred, and discontent.

" In this world a woman or a man is an envious person,
" jealous of the prosperity, honour, and respect enjoyed by
" others, and dissatisfied and annoyed at perceiving these
" marks of honour conferred on others ; this person, in conse-
" quence of the conduct to which he has been so fully
" accustomed, upon the dissolution of his frame by death,
" will be born in hell, wretched, miserable, and tormented ;
" or if he be not born in hell, but if he again become a human
" being, wherever he may be born he will be destitute of
" power and influence.   The path which leads to a destitution
" of influence is to be envious, jealous, dissatisfied, and
" annoyed at the prosperity, honour, and respect enjoyed by
" others.

" In this world a woman or a man is not an envious per-
" son ; is neither jealous, dissatisfied, nor annoyed at the pros-
" perity, honour, or respect enjoyed by others ; this person, in
" consequence of the conduct to which he has been so fully
" accustomed, upon the dissolution of his frame by death will
" be born in heaven in a state of happiness ; or if he be not
" born in heaven, but if he again become a human being,
" wherever he may be born he will be possessed of extensive
" power.   The path for the attainment of great power is to be

2

"free from envy, and to be neither jealous, dissatisfied, nor
"annoyed at the prosperity, honour, or respect enjoyed by
"others.

"In this world a woman or a man does not give to Samanas
"and Brahmans meat, drink, garments, a conveyance for
"travelling, flowers, perfumes, ointments, a couch, a cham-
"ber, a lamp; this person, in consequence of the conduct to
"which he has become so fully accustomed, upon the disso-
"lution of his frame by death will be born in hell, wretched,
"miserable, and tormented; or if he be not born in hell, but
"if he again become a human being, wherever he may be
"born he will be poor. The part leading to poverty is to
"omit giving to Samanas and Brahmans meat, drink, cloth-
"ing, a conveyance, flowers, perfumes, and ointments, a
"couch, a chamber, and a lamp.

"In this world a woman or a man gives to Samanas or
"Brahmans meat, drink, clothing, a conveyance, flowers,
"perfumes, and ointments, a couch, a chamber, and a lamp;
"this person, in consequence of the conduct to which he has
"become so fully accustomed, upon the dissolution of his
"frame by death will be born in heaven in the enjoyment of
"happiness; or if he be not born in heaven, but if he again
"become a human being, wherever he may be born he will
"be rich. The path for the attainment of riches is to give to
"Samanas or Brahmans meat, drink, clothing, a conveyance,
"flowers, perfumes, and ointments, a couch, a chamber, and
"a lamp.

"In this world a woman or a man is proud and haughty,
"not worshipping those who ought to be worshipped, not
"rising from their seat in the presence of those who should
"be thus reverenced, not requesting those to be seated who
"are worthy of that honour, nor removing out of the path
"when eminent persons approach, not treating with hospi-
"tality, respect, and reverence those who should be thus
"respected; this person, in consequence of the conduct to
"which he has been fully accustomed, upon the dissolution
"of his body by death will be born in hell, wretched, miser-
"able, and tormented, or if he be not born in hell, but if he
"again become a human being, wherever he may be born he
"will be of ignoble birth. The path which leads to an
"ignoble birth is this: the being proud and haughty, not
"worshipping those who ought to be worshipped, not rising
"up in the presence of those who should be thus reverenced,
"not offering a seat to those worthy of that honour, not giving
"the path to eminent persons, not treating with hospitality,
"respect, and reverence those who should be thus respected.

"In this world a woman or a man is not proud nor haughty,
"but worship those who ought to be worshipped, rises up in
"the presence of those who should be thus reverenced, re-
"quests them to be seated who are worthy of that honour,
"gives the path to eminent persons, and treats with hospi-
"tality, respect, and reverence those who should be thus res-
"pected ; this person, in consequence of the conduct to which
"he has been so fully accustomed, upon the dissolution of
"his frame by death will be born in heaven in the enjoyment
"of happiness ; or if he be not born in heaven, but if he
"again become a human being, wherever he may be born he
"will be of honourable parentage. The path for obtaining
"honourable parentage is this, not to be proud nor haughty,
"to worship those who ought to be worshipped, to rise up in
"the presence of those who should be thus reverenced, to re-
"quest them to be seated who are worthy of that honour, to
"give the path to eminent persons, and to treat with hospi-
"tality, respect, and reverence those who should be thus res-
"pected.

"In this world a woman or a man does not wait upon a
"Samana or a Brahman to enquire of him saying, sir, what
"constitutes merit and what demerit ? What actions are
"criminal and what are innocent ? What things ought to be
"done and what left undone ? What actions are those which,
"if done, will produce protracted distress and wretchedness?
"Or what are those which will be productive of lengthened
"tranquillity and happiness ? This person, in consequence
"of the conduct to which he has become so fully accustomed,
"upon the dissolution of his frame by death will be born in
"hell, wretched, miserable, and tormented ; or if he be not
"born in hell, but if he again become a human being wher-
"ever he may be born he will be destitute of wisdom. The
"path to mental imbecility is this, to neglect to wait upon a
"Samana or Brahman for the purpose of enquiring of him
"saying, sir, what constitutes merit and what demerit ?
"What actions are criminal and what innocent ? What
"things ought to be done and what left undone ? What
"actions are those which, is done, will cause me protracted
"distress and wretchedness, or what are those which will be
"productive of lengthened tranquillity and happiness ?

"In this world a woman or a man waits upon a Samana or
"Brahman and enquires of him, saying, sir, what constitutes
"merit and what demerit ? What actions are criminal and
"what are innocent ? What things ought to be done and
"what left undone ? What actions are those which, if done,
"will cause me protracted distress and wretchedness ? Or

" what are those which will be productive of lengthened tran-
" quillity and happiness ? This person, in consequence of
" the conduct to which he has become so fully accustomed,
" upon the dissolution of his frame by death will be born in
" heaven in the enjoyment of happiness. Or if he be not born
" in heaven, but if he again become a human being, wher-
" ever he may be born he may be possessed of great wisdom.
" The path for the attainment of great wisdom is this : to
" wait upon a Samana or Brahman for the purpose of enquiry,
" saying, sir, what constitutes merit and what demerit ?
" What actions are criminal and what are innocent ? What
" things ought to be done and what left undone ? What ac-
" tions are those which, if done, will cause me protracted dis-
" tress and wretchedness ? Or what are those which will be
" productive or lengthened tranquillity and happiness ? Thus
" young man the conduct (or path) productive of short-
" ness of life leads to a short life ; the conduct productive of
" length of life leads to longevity. The conduct productive of
" continued sickness leads to a state of disease, and that which
" is productive of ugliness leads to a disgusting appearance ;
" and that which is productive of comeliness leads to personal
" beauty. The conduct productive of little influence leads to
" a state destitute of power, and that productive of great influ-
" ence leads to a state of great authority. The conduct pro-
" ductive of want leads to a state of poverty, and that pro-
" ductive of wealth leads to opulence. The conduct pro-
" ductive of low birth leads to ignoble parentage, and that
" productive of honour leads to a noble birth. The conduct
" productive of ignorance leads to a state of mental imbecil-
" ity, and that productive of knowledge leads to a state of
" wisdom. Living beings receive the results of their own
" conduct ; their conduct forms their inheritance, their birth,
" their relationship, their cirumstances in life ; conduct
" apportions to living beings prosperity or adversity." When
Guatama ended the discourse Subha warmly expressed his
admiration and embraced the Buddhist faith.

NOTES ON BUDDHIST LAW

MARRIAGE

A translation of the text of the Chapter on Marriage in the Manoo
Wonnana Dhammathat as edited by Moung Tet Too in Burmese,
with Notes by John Jardine, Esq., Bo. C.S., Judicial Commissioner, British Burma, and Remarks by Dr. E. Forchhammer,
Professor of Pali.

S. 105   When sons, daughters, grandchildren, great-grandchildren
and male slaves and female slaves are not given in marriage before
the completion of the sixteenth year, the sexual act shall not be called
a fault.

Note.—Much of this chapter is based on the ancient Hindu law : *e g.*, in the
code of Manu the following text shows that a girl should be married before
puberty :—

"Reprehensible is the father who gives not his daughter in marriage at the proper time." Whether the three Burmese forms of marriage are derived from the
Hindus I am unable to conjecture : the absence of distinct ceremony, such as the
taking of the seven steps, and the absence of sacramental ideas, make it more
difficult to determine the exact point at which the status of husband and wife
begins At Hindu law there was some difference between the nobler and meaner
forms as to irrevocability. !*See* text 177 and others in Colebrooke, Vol. 2.) The
habits of the people in British Burma are changing under the influence of British
laws and Courts. which have interfered with the *patria potestas*, the old suit for
seduction, the right to specific performance of contract of marriage, the pecuniary
amercement for rape, and the law of maintenance. I mention this because in
British Burma many people speak as if the law of the country were still the same,
as that in force in the Kingdom of Burma. As to the jural view, of marriage
being an institution as well as a contract, and the power of Hindu parents to con-
gract their children in marriage, see the judgment of Westropp C.J. in "Sidlin-
tapa *vs* Sidava, " I. L. R. 2 Bombay, 624.

S. 107.   If a young man has sexual connection with an adult
woman (ဥ၄း၀ တ္), he should take her for his wife, and if, not being
on good terms, he wishes not to remain, he shall pay the price of the
sexual connection ; but as the price of a putsoe (skirt) is lowered by
its being already stitched so *judging the price of the sexual connection*
according to the four pa lesas, the payment to be given should be
two-thirds of the price.

Remarks.—Ma-ha-be-da-tha-law-yet or rather *Mahapades layyat*, mean the four
Mahapadesas (မဟာပဒေသလေးရပ်). The Burmans, in appraising the value
of anything bought or acquired, will say : "Considering the *time* (i. kála),
the *place* ii, desa). (when and where a thing has been bought or acquired or an
event occurred), its intrinsic value as a piece of *property* (iii, dhanam), and the
price (iv, aggham) at which it has been acquired, its value can be put down at
such and such a price. This is called making the value or price of a thing according
to the four padesas or Mahapadesas (kála, desa, dhanam, aggham). I would
translate the passage thus : (but, as the price of a putsoe is lowered by being
already stitched (a ဥ၄း၀ တ္ is worth less than a virgin), so judging, the price
of the sexual connection according to the four padesas, the payment to be given
should be two-thirds of the price.

S. 108. If a man abandons his wife and becomes a " rahan, " and if another man takes that man's wife, there is no fault ; but if the first husband, knowing that fact, beccmes a layman, she shall be handed over to him : in this way if a man repeatedly becomes a rahan eight times and alternately becomes a layman, the wife is acquitted of fault ; she has a right to live with a *second* husband if she wishes, but seven repetitions must be waited for. Thus it is ordained in some olden scriptures.

Note.—The mode of admission to the monastic order of rahans is fully described in Bishop Bigandet's *Legend of Guutama.* In Bk. 5, s. 17 of the *Menu Kyay* it is said that the wife need only wait seven days and may then take another husband, while the rahan becoming layman again after seven days has no right to reclaim her These rules are embodied in Sparks' Code. In the Pali and in s. 140 of the *Manoo Thara Shwe Myeen* the rule is stated as in the *Wonnana.* Two Native Judges, Oo Wike and Moung Htine, say the rule of the *Menu Kyay* is conformable to present custom. Moung Htine reconciles the two rules as both implying that the man is not to be considered as a rahan until he has shown his vocation to the holy order by living at least seven days in the mo iastery, or by adopting its rules at last after being attracted several times to return to the world. Moung Htine adds that the Abbot will not receive a shin or postulant, if a married man, until after inquiry it is ascertained that he is not in debt and that his wife has no objections.

Remarks.—The Burmese translation gives the Pali correctly, but I am unable to trace the passage in "olden scriptures" or anywhere else. The rule in *Menu Kyay,* Bk. 5, s. 17, is generally given. S. 108 does not occur in the *Wagaru.*
A man may become a rahan, or enter the monastic order, though his wife objects ; but a wife *must* have the consent of her husband if she wishes to become a nun : numerous instances occur in the *Dhammapadaratthu* and the *Jatakas.*

S. 109. Sons and daughters already given away in marriage (ပြီးစွာ၍) are each individually responsible ; and even if there is a loss, the husband and wife, two persons, cannot claim from the mother and father ; and even if the girl be the daughter of a king, only the husbands to whom the mother and father have given *the girls* possess control : other persons do not possess such control. If the wife is lost, or is destroyed, the husband bears the husband's burden, and if the husband is lost, or destroyed, the wife bears it.

S. 110. If daughters given in marriage and living in a separate house should fall ill and the husband does not cure her, and the mother and father give and send her eatables, and the mother and father cure her, and the sores leave her and disappear, then, if *the husband* wants that wife back, he must pay to the mother and father all the expenses of the illness.

Note.—The husband is bound to maintain and cherish a diseased wife (*see* paragraph 57 of my first Note on marringe and section 115 below).

S. 111. There are eight motives for giving daughters in marriage—

(1) the assertion that the man is of high family ;
(2) a promise to make presents in return ;
(3) a promise to do some business or other ;
(4) a promise to discharge some important service ;
(5) the fact that threats have been spoken ;
(6) a promise to do service inside the house ;
(7) a promise to cure a disease ; and
(8) mutual wish.

Note.—This statement of motives inducing the parents of the girl to give her in marriage is not found in the *Menu Kyay*, and much of the following sections is also not found there. The reader will notice the application of the maxim *factum valet*, the dislike to disturb an union after consummation has taken place, the endeavour otherwise to defeat fraud, and to make false pretences the subject of damages. My present impression is that this and the cognate sections deal with Burman customs rather than Hindu law.

S. 112. The daughter is given in marriage because of the statement in the presence of the elders that the *man* is of high race. If not of high race as stated, there is a right to take back the daughter.

Note.—The law defining differences of rank and some curious ceremonial provisions are found in the beginning of the 6th Book of the *Menu Kyay*; and there are many allusions elsewhere. As regards the scale in which damage are calculated, see s. 9 of that book

S. 113. Because it is promised in the presence of the elders that presents will be made in return, the daughter who is loved is given *to the lover.* If he gives according to his promise the presents are got, if he does not give they are not got, because the girl has already had sexual connection.

Note.—The translation is difficult, but the meaning seems to me the same as in section 16 of the 6th Book of the *Menu Kyay*, namely, that if the girl's parents do not demand the promised presents at the time of the giving (paiza) of the girl, they shall not afterwards obtain them. The marriage having been consummated is not to be annulled for mere breach of contract with the girl's parents. See also sections 20, 23, and 24, where the same reason is put forth.

S. 114. Because, in the presence of the elders, a promise to do some business was made, if the girl who is loved is given, three years' service must be done to the mother and father in the mother and father's house.

Note —This and the following section differ somewhat from s. 20 of Bk. 6 of the *Menu Kyay*, where there is no fixed period of service, but special contracts are referred to. S. 117 is an abstract statement of the last part of that s. 20 to which perhaps the reference is made. S. 38 of Bk. 12 deals with separation from wives obtained in return for benefits conferred, namely, saving of life, curing disease, relieving in trouble, or assisting in business. The benefactor is not to make a claim and on that account, the obligation being apparently cancelled by the marriage.

S. 115. If because of a promise in the presence of the elders to perform some important service *the daughter* is given, the giving is a good *giving.* But if again there is not a willingness to *give the girl,* the mother and father must pay the price (ကိုယ်သိုး) of the daughter's body to the son of that good man.

Remarks.—The Pali text runs thus : Karissam para sammukhe, vatva dinna sudinnakam sace asamachandakam, aggham tassa dadenti te. (Lit. trans.) "It shall "be 'done' in the presence of others having said, the given a good given. If "unequally desiring, the price of her they give to him." If because of a promise in the presence of others to perform a service (the daughter) is given, the giving is a good (giving) ; but if they should desire it otherwise (or change their mind), they must give him the price of her (body). There is nothing in the Pali text of " a good man's son."

S. 116. On account of threats there was a giving of a daughter. Former wise men have pointed out that, when the fears have ceased, that daughter may be taken back.

Note.—Compare with s. 9 of Bk. 2 of the *Menu Kyay*, where the doctrine is stated in the following words:—" Gifts made through fears may afterwards be " taken back by force, and people will not scorn the recoverer. Why shalt they ," be so taken back, and the persons taking them escape censure? Because they " were given through fear of force " Some limitations and applications will be found in s. 3 of Bk. 8.

S. 117. A daughter is given because service is being done. If there has been sexual intercourse, wise men have pointed out that that daughter should by right be the good man's son's wife

Note —In ss 19 and 20 of Bk. 2 of the *Menu Kyay* there is a curious statement of the law about doctors' fees and what was expected from the doctor.

S. 118. A daughter is given over (ေဝးအပ်) because disease has been cured. If sexual intercourse has taken place, and if after the disease has disappeared *the daughter* is not given, the value of that daughter's body shall be given to the medical man.

S. 119. If a daughter is given on account of a mutual consent, he is entitled to get whatever was mutually consented to (by the parents? J.J.). If sexual connection takes place, there is a right to own. If sexual connection does not take place, *he* is entitled to half the price (တန်ဖိုး) (tanbo) of the daughter. If sexual connection takes place with a man with the consent of the daughter, and if the mother and father wish to avoid shame, they should give their daughter *to the man.*

S. 120. If both the mothers and fathers in the presence of other persons point out the son and daughter and promise to connect themselves (*i.e.*, the two parental couples) by the giving *in marriage* of the children, the two parental couples should give *in marriage* according to the promise. If even either the son or daughter thus pointed out dies, another son or daughter shall be given. It is not right if this is not done. If the *surviving* son or daughter is given to another person (instead of to the substitute of the deceased, J. J.), half the presents (အတွင်း) shall be taken back or snatched. Such should be the previous understanding (about presents?', and it is right that the promise should be carried into execution. Such a promise has never been broken.

Note —This stringent section must be studied along with the more equitable rules of s. 30 of Bk. 6 of the *Menu Kyay* Dhamma that, where exceptions are made in favour of previous engagements of substitutes and of young people who object to marry each other. The language in both these sections shows that there was a difference of legal opinion. The obligation of a promise solemnly made might, according to s 21 of Bk. 2 of the *Menu Kyay*, be enforced by penal sanction. But, in the absence of express promise, it is difficult to find any sufficient grounds for insisting on the giving of the substitute, who might be already contracted in marriage to some other family. The parents of the survivor of the two young people might naturally desire to get the costly presents promised by the other side but not actually given at the time of the contract and before the actual giving in marriage, and might therefore find it convenient to insist on a substitute. But the reasons against allowing such a course are evident from the section in the *Menu Kyay*. Moung Wike, the aged Sitkeh of Pegu, reconciles the two Dhammathats by supposing, what the language seems to indicate, that the real contract between the two sets of parents was to unite the two families by a marriage, there being no limitations about any particular child. Moung Htine approves the doctrines of the *Menu Kyay* as the correct one. Section 120 of the *Wonnana* seems to me to give a vivid picture of the betrothal and is an example of the contract being made by the parents (*see* " Sidlingapa *vs.* Sidava," L. R. 2 Bombay, 624).

I quote the following texts 170 and 172 from Colebrooke's Digest of Hindu law :—

Manu.—The damsel indeed whose husband shall die after troth verbally plighted but before consummation, his brother shall take in marriage.

If a nuptial gratuity have actually been given to a damsel, and he who gave it should die before marriage, the damsel shall be married to his brother if she consent.

The Specific Relief Act following decisions of the Indian High Court forbids the Courts to direct specific performance of a contract to marry : but in British Burma suits for damages for breach of such a contract are occasionally brought by Buddhist women.

S. 121. The mother and father should not give their daughter before the giving and receiving of the presents ; if they happen so to give, such giving is wrong, for the daughter has endured sexual connection. The son-in-law gives the presents ; there is a right to such presents only as have been given. If the articles are not given, those articles shall not be got, for those articles were not given beforehand. Such is the order.

S. 122. After the mother and father have placed their son and daughter in marriage (literally in a house of their own) and put them amongst established married people (*i.e.*, enlisting them in the category of people with households), if they once again take them and give them in marriage, such an act is not that of mother and father, but of other persons. If a daughter already given by mother and father goes wrong with another man, and if the husband to whom she was given has had no sexual intercourse, that daughter shall return the presents given for sexual intercourse. If sexual intercourse has already taken place *with the husband, she* shall return double the presents. A woman obtained through a go-between (*i.e.*, a negotiator or broker of marriages who brings eligible persons to notice of each other or the parents, J.J.), a woman obtained by mutual consent, a woman given by mother and father, with such three kinds of women there may be sexual connection. If there is not a wish to remain together, the price of the body shall be given.

If the man does not wish to remain, he shall not get the presents and articles ; in other words, *the girl* may return to her parents' house : after the period of three years that woman becomes free from the status of being the wife of that good man's son. if the daughter given by the mother and father ceases to like the husband, double the presents must be taken.

Note.—The matters here discussed are mentioned in the *Menu Kyay.* As regards the first sentence, the following extract from s. 30 of Bk. 6 states the rule about emancipation of women by marriage:—" If a woman be a widow " or divorced from her husband and she marry the man of her choice, her parents, " guardians, or relatives have no right to interfere to prevent it : let the woman who " has already had a husband take the man of her choice. If she has never had a " husband, she shall have no right to take one without the consent of her parents or " guardians." The second sentence relates to the subject discussed in s. 16 of Bk. 6, where a different rule of compensation is given. Then the three kinds of marriages are mentioned as in the other books (*see* my first Note).

The remainder of the section under comment is obscure. It appears to me to mix s. 17 of Bk. 5 with s. 15 of Bk. 6 of the *Menu Kyay,*—*see* paragraph 54 of my first Note and paragraph 29 of my second Note, as well as paragraph 135 of the *Wonnana* below. The general rule derived from Hindu law seems to be that a wife deserted by her husband after cohabitation, or a wife who after cohabitation deserts him, as often happens through quarrels, and goes back to her parents' house, is not at liberty to marry any other man until a period of three years has expired. As stated by Sandford, J. at page 16 of his Rulings, "three years' absence, with "neglect on the part of the husband to provide the wife with the means of subsis- "tence, is required to give the wife the right of re-marriage." The exceptions will be found in the different texts. The restriction is important in the discussion about *ex-parte* divorce without any cause, and being apparently unknown to many Burmese women, their refusal to acknowledge their husbands after an angry departure to the parents' house often leads to murder. The rule is reiterated in s. 165 below, and is also stated in the *Manoo Thara Shwe Myeen* as follows in s. 139:—"A person given in marriage by the mother and father after "living in a separate house goes back to the mother and father's house. Then if "*the husband* does not for about three years give anything for purposes of clothing "and maintenance, she after the three years becomes free from going up the house "(*i.e.*, from the status of wife, if she so chooses, J.J.). If the man has to go to a "battle, six years ; if in search of charitable deeds, eight years ; if in pursuit of "learning, ten years must be awaited. Beyond the abovementioned periods *the* "*wife* is free ; within the abovementioned periods there is no freedom. If taken "captive within the abovementioned period, the person who gets *the woman* is the "one entitled. The reason is because *the woman* was taken away from the battle- "field." The word translated "captive" is *thonglct* ; and in putting a sense on the last part of the above extract from the *Shwe Myeen* I have been guided by s. 35 of Bk. 12 of the *Menu Kyay*, where the thong-ya, pan-ya, and let-ya wives, or wives taken in war, are described. See also Bk. 7, s. 25, at page 198 of Richardson's edition. S. 274 of the *Shwe Myeen* distinctly asserts that if the wife of a captive husband marries another man within the period, then if the second husband knew of the former husband's captivity, the former husband gets back his wife and the other man loses the presents. Both s. 275 of the *Shwe Myeen* and s. 716 of the *Wonnana* assert the right of the owner to recover his children, wife, goods, and slaves when they have been taken in war. S. 33 of Bk. 6 of the *Menu Kyay* is also clear on the same subject.

I must here remark that the *Wonnana* and *Shwe Myeen* contain hardly any allusions to the three kinds of wives taken in war. Some learned Burmans have assured me that the *Menu Kyay* deals with circumstances caused by wars between the Burmans and Arakanese ; and Dr. Forchhammer has thrown out a suggestion that the conquest of the Talaings by the Burmans under Alompra may have greatly affected both law and custom. Some future scholar will perhaps avail himself of these hints in settling the age of the *Menu Kyay*. As corresponding enactments are not to be found in the Hindu Shasters, the Burmans are likely enough to be right in giving a recent and local origin to that part of Bk. 12 of the *Menu Kyay*. See Dr. Forchhammer's remarks on s. 144 below.

I am inclined to think that the section under comment implies that each of the three forms of marriage is valid, and that the consent of the young people being immaterial when the marriage is of the first and most honourable form, *i.e.*, by giving of the parents, they, the young couple are bound by it. There is no mention in the *Wonnana* or the *Shwe Myeen* of the doctrine * of s. 15 of Bk. 6 of the *Menu Kyay* that the girl may annul the contract by running away three times from her husband's to her parents' house, or the similar doctrine of s. 22 that she may select her own husband before marriage by eloping with him three times. (*See* paragraph 9 and following paragraphs of my first Note.) In this and other respects already noted the *Menu Kyay* is more liberal. The maxim that the parents are owners of the children is suspended when they cannot control the children. On this point see s. 127 below. Even s. 106 of the *Wonnana* implies that the parental power of contracting should be exercised before the children are 16 years of age. Any one who discusses such points with Burmans will find it difficult at first to get a clear answer to the question whether the contract made by the parents can create the status of husband and wife where one of the children absolutely refuses consent. The ultimate reply is usually in the negative. Similar questions have puzzled the commentators on the Hindu law : and difficult cases about the commencement of the married status may easily arise. Section 23 of the *Menu Kyay* deals with an irregular and lawless proceeding, which, if the girl who elopes is under that age, might, even under our Penal Code, be criminal. In a case

---

* Dr. Forchhammer states that there is nothing about this doctrine in the *Wagaru* or *Wini Tsaya Paka Thani*. It is, in his belief, an instance of an exclusively Burmese (not Talaing or Arakanese) custom, constituting a source of Buddhist or Burmese law.

recently before me from Pegu the parents and elders arranged with the young couple's consent that they should live together and become man and wife, and were doubtless scandalized when the young lover was convicted and sent to prison. The section shows that a judicial interposition preceded the act of marriage. The words of this section and of section 15 about the girl given in marriage against her will do convey the impression that, even after consummation, the woman has a right to insist on divorce against the will of the man. S. 15 is the case of a girl who has persistently objected to her parents' choice. S. 23 is that of a girl who has not waited till her twentieth year till her judgment is matured, and after elopement has lived with the man as her husband. The first case is expressly that of young people never before married ; the second implies the same thing. The question arises whether these are exceptions to a general rule that *ex-parte* divorce may not occur except for valid cause, or whether a reluctant consent by the unwilling partner is to be assumed a implied.

The same sort of difficulty arises in the section under comment about the words '' If there is not a wish to remain together, the price of the body shall be given.'' The context seems to show that some fraudulent proceeding is meant like those mentioned before and after the statement of the well-known law of marriage. As regards the case of elopement, ss. 21 and 22 of Bk. 6 of the *Menu Kyay* show that the lover had no inherent right to re-claim the girl back from the parents' house, unless she gave a fresh consent to live with him ; his act is of the nature of a fraud on the parents (see s. 28), and possibly he deceived the young girl.

S. 123. The mother and father in the negotiations point out the young daughter. If at the time of the giving the elder daughter is given, the good man's son has a right to both those daughters. Otherwise if, after sexual embracing of the daughter actually given, he does not want her, the presents shall be returned. The reason of this is that the mother and father had fraudulent intent.

Note.—This case is similar to one described in s. 16 of Bk. 6 of the *Menu Kyay*, where the wrong daughter is fraudulently introduced into the bed-chamber.

S. 124. He who, in spite of a promise that a *girl* shall be given him, has sexual embracings with another daughter or with a slave, is not entitled to get the daughter who was promised.

S. 125. If that daughter does not wish for that man, the presents shall not be given back. The parents and the parents-in-law have been put to shame ; therefore he is said to be a fraudulent man and is said to change about like a dog.

Note.—This and the preceding section may be compared with s. 16 of Bk. 6 of the *Menu Kyay*, where the scandalously unfaithful bridegroom not only loses his bride, but is expected to marry the other woman.

S. 126. If before having sexual connection *with the girl* given by the mother and father, the man has connection with other women, that good man's daughter shall not allege that her husband has been stolen.

Otherwise if a man, without inquiry or information, falls in love with another man's daughter endowed with beauty and performs great and small businesses, and at the end of three years the mother and father, differing in their respective wishes, give that young girl to another man, and that *first* young man falls in love with some other woman, that mother and father should give a suit of man's clothes, a suit of woman's clothes, rice and curry pots, and the articles which he had brought to the man who served for three years ; thus learned men should decide.

If the man does not fall in love and if he does not get that young daughter, wise men of old have pointed out that half the price of the daughter's body should be given.

Note.—The above may be considered with ss. 17 and 20 of Bk. 6 of the *Menu Kyay*, where higher compensation is given. Why the period of three years' service should be fixed is not apparent. Can it be a confusion about the period after which a deserted wife may re-marry? Moung Htine says no : he says the practice of serving for a wife used to be common : the three years was a fair period of probation as the youngster was an ignoramus at starting. (See also s. 24.) The case of the jilted suitor falling in love with some other girl is a new refinement.

S. 127. .I —Parents who possess a daughter are entitled to take and keep betel, tea (lit-stone or brick tea, *i.e.*, pressed tea), fruits, flowers, eatables, offered (to them) by (as many as) ten men.

II.—When (the parents) have arranged about the marriage (of their daughter with a man) they may accept presents (from him); if they take (the presents) but give (the daughter) to another man, they are guilty of having defrauded (the first man) of his connubial rights.

III.—If (the parents) have taken the presents, but the daughter not wishing [to become the wife of the man selected by the parents, runs away, another daughter may be given (in her stead) ; if (another daughter is) not (given), all the presents (given) must be returned] provided sexual intercourse has not taken place ; if sexual intercourse has taken place, twofold (the amount of the presents) must (be given).

Note.—The above is in Pali, and the reader will notice the same sort of vagueness as attends most answers given by either Englishmen or Burmans whom he may question on the subject. It is not easy to get any precise answers to the inquiry whether the parents can contract the marriage of the children without the children's consent. As the husband and wife inherit from each other, the answer is of the utmost importance. S. 127 would seem to show that some overt act, something more than mere mutual promises and giving and receiving of presents was required to create the status of husband and wife.

With the above may be compared the following sections of Book 6 of the *Menu Kyay* :—

S. 17. If parents have received large bridal presents, and do not give their daughter to the giver of them, but to a rich man, they shall return to him double. Why is this ? Because they have departed from their engagement.

S. 19. If parents have a maiden daughter, and the parents of several young men approving of her shall separately make presents of betel, tea, gold, silver or cloth, and demand her in marriage, and the maiden's parents accept them with a promise that, if she is willing, they will give her in marriage, should the maiden on consideration approve of the person who first or last made the presents, or any one of them, let her be given to him ; and if the parents of the other young men demand back their presents on the ground that she has not been given to their son, they shall not recover them. Why is this ? Because it was stipulated she should be given to the one whom she should choose ; her parents have a right to keep the presents. If the agreement was not made thus, but they receive the presents of one saying they will oblige her to marry (their son), that the engagement with them is final, and if after this they give her to another, let them return all the presents.

Here again, something more than mere promises seem required to create the status of husband and wife. I have consulted two Burman Judges but they cannot explain s 19. It may possibly be derived from the Hindu Svayamvara, but I suspect it is really a rule from Burmese custom.

Remarks.—The Pali original of 127 of the *Wunnana* is as follows :—

I.—Mātāpitā sadhitara dinne ambulasilaje
     Phale pupphe bhojane, gāheyyum dasaposinam.

II.—Atha sanketakādikam katvā gāhiyya dinnakam
Sace gāheyya aññinā kāmadosasaman dade

III.—Sunkam gahiyya sadhita, n'iccha palāyi aññakam
Dhitam dadeyya, no sace, sabbasunkam na sevitam
Sevitam pana dvegunam.

It must be noted that the word *silajo*, verse I, is not a classical Pali word ; the word has been framed in Burma to give a name to the pressed " brick t a " (sila-jo, stone-produced), found in Burmese bazaars and prepared chiefly by the Paloungs in Upper Burma. The first verse has certainly been composed in Burma to suit Burmese customs and verses II and III are adverse to the spirit of Hindu law and society. The passage does not occur in the *Wagaru*.

Swayamvara does not appear to me to fall under s. 127. In the above three verses parents' are represented as receiving suitors for their daughters and negotiating matches upon their own and exclusive responsibility, entailing dishonour and loss upon the parents in case of non-compliance with their wish on the part of the daughter. Swayamvara is the selection of a husband by the damsel herself ; she becomes a party to the matrimonial contract ; the interest of parents or guardians need not be consulted, their compliance is not required, and any protest is legally ineffectual according to Hindu law. Swayamvara is sometimes allowed to girls neglected by their parents and guardians, because a girl is dishonored when not betrothed at attaining puberty According to the Apastamba, swayamvara takes place in case " a (marriageable) girl (who is not given in marriage) shall a low " three monthly periods to pass, and afterwards unite herself of her own will to " a man of her choice, giving up the ornaments received from her family. He " who fails to give a girl in marriage before puberty commits sin. "

S. 128. If some one from a distant place makes presents and solicits for the girl, and the mother and father receive the presents, and if that girl has had sexual connection with another man, or is pregnant or is barren (ြ[ေသ5), or a leper, or deaf or dumb, or deformed in a member, such defect must be told to the person *soliciting*. If it is not told, and the two marry (စိ:ြာ:), and *the man* says he is unwilling to remain *with her*, the only thing which the mother and father in charge of the presents ought to do is to give them back. But if he knows or sees *the defect* and does not speak, and after sexual connection with her expresses his unwillingness, he shall forfeit the presents, however numerous they may be.

Note.—The corresponding provision of the *Menu Kyay* is found in s. 18 of Bk. 6 ; see also my note to s 156 in the chapter on divorce. In this s. 128 is embodied one of the commonest maxims of our own law and equity. The Hindu Manu authorizes the King to fine the person who gives a blemished girl in marriage. " If any man give a faulty damsel in marriage, without disclosing " her blemish, the husband may annul that act of her ill-minded giver. "

S. 129. If husband and wife given in marriage by mother and father dwell in a seeparate house and are unwilling *to cohabit*, and in presence of elders divide *the property* and get divorced (တွာလောၐါ) and again agree, neither the husband nor wife can be blamed for breach of the written award ; in other words, if the daughter has removed to the house of her father and mother and eats and drinks there, and if the husband and wife by mutual consent wish to live together, but the mother and father do not consent, they have a right to take back their daughter. The reason for this is that they treat her as covered by their breast (meaning under their care, J.J.).

If a son is called from his father-in-law's house to perform his duties *in his own father's house*, even if he dies, his parents and *relations* are without fault.

Note.—I cannot support the doctrine of this section out of the *Menu Kyay.*
In Bk. 0, s 30, it is said :—"If children do not minister to their parents
"but leave them and live separately, let all their property be taken from them,
"and they may be punished criminally to the extent of six hundred stripes with
"a rattan." But in the next sentence the same treatment is ordained for the husband or wife who leaves the other. See also my note to s. 122 above.

S. 130. A man through having a suit is reduced to poverty. He
says, "Conduct the suit all of ye, I will give my daughter." A certain person without any particular motive conducts the suit. The
suit being finished (or won?), if the daughter and the mother and
father jointly consent, he is entitled to fulfilment of the promise. If
there is not a joint consent, the price of the girl's body shall be
given.

Note.—Similar provision will be found in ss. 94, 96, and 99 of *Thara Shwe
Myeen* : but this and the next case are not noticed in the *Menu Kyay.* For the law
regarding pleaders, see s. 20 of Bk. 2 of that Dhammathat.

S. 131. There happening to be a suit, some one says (or
stipulates) *to conduct it,* and before performance of the proposal the
suitor gives his young daughter. That good man's son, being
unsuccessful in the matter promised (having tried and failed to win
the suit, J.J.), through shame abandons (the girl already given him,
J.J.) and goes away.

Another man in the same manner conducts the suit. If when
the suit is won, the first man comes and says, "She is my wife,"
which of the twain is entitled to her as wife? The second man
alone is entitled to that young woman : the bragging liar who ran
away should not get her.

Note.—The fact in this case were that the girl was actually given in the
most honourable form of marriage by her father, who believed that the man
would fulfil his promise of conducting the suit He ran away without fulfilling
the promise and the girl was given to another person. The first husband cannot
claim her as his wife in the case stated. What would have happened if the second
marriage had not taken place we can only conjecture. The above looks like an
actual decision : and I explain it by the doctrine of mutual consent shown by the
first husband by conduct and by the wife by acquiescence and second marriage.
It would be inconsistent with all the other sections to suppose that the first
husband could terminate the marriage or gain any rights against the wife by
means of abandonment or other tortious behaviour. It would not, in my opinion,
be inconsistent to hold that the wife so abandoned might acquire rights against
the husband. Moung Htine informs me that where the parties are in the same
village and the husband shows by words or conduct a determination to abandon
the wife, she may contract a second marriage before the expiry of the period of
three years discussed under s 122 The intention of the absent husband cannot
be so easily inferred.

In discussing s 131 with Moung Htine, a Judge at Prome, I put two new
test cases in order to get a precise understanding. Suppose the first husband
after abandoning the wife, flees away, and while so fleeing is stung by a serpent
and dies before the wife has given him up or re-married Does the wife inherit from
the deceased husband by force of the well-known maxim that husbands and wives
inherit from each other ? Moung Htine's reply was that she does.

Again, supposing that the runaway husband comes back and the wife,
not having re-married or given him up but being destitute of subsistence, applies
to a Magistrate for an order of maintenance under the Code of Criminal Procedure.
The husband answers that she is not his wife. Is that a good plea ? Moung
Htine's reply was in the negative, on the ground that a mere tortious abandonment not subsequently ratified by the wife does not put an end to the status of
husband and wife. These responses are, in my opinion, correct. Even a man who

renounces the world by becoming a rahan does not at once terminate the marriage ; and Moung Htine says the other pyitshins or monks would not admit him if he merely put on the yellow robe in order to divorce himself from his wife Much less, than, can a layman acting on base motives effect a divorce by merely running away. Such maxims as that of the wife being the heir of the husband really belong to a sound system of jurisprudence : the reason for it, as given in the Dhammathats quoted in the judgment on inheritance given in the appendix, are that the wife did her part in taking care of the property, and she is even for this reason entitled to greater rights than any of the children or all the children together.

In s. 131 the *Wonnana* does not make it quite clear whether the power of ratifying a desertion belongs to the daughter or her parents. In s. 135 it is vested in the mother I have noticed the more liberal dictates of the *Menu Kyay*. But the difference of the two books as to the girl's power of contracting does not affect the above argument.

S. 132. A man says to a mother and father, " I have no wife. " That mother and father, believing that it is really true that he has none, give him their daughter in marriage. If afterwards a son or wife turns up, whether one or two persons, children of that good man's son must be given. Then he may stay with his new wife. If there are no sons and daughters, they may live together only when the greater wife makes her husband over to his new parents-in-law : if she does not make him over, they cannot live together and the presents cannot be received.

Note.—This section of the *Wonnana* has no counterpart in the *Menu Kyay*, and the words being obscure, I give the corresponding passage in the *Manoo Thara Shwe Myeen*, s. 116 :—" Because a man says 'I have no wife' a daughter "is given to him. Afterwards a wife or son turns up. One or two of his children "shall be given to the new parent-in-law : then only can he live with the new "wife. If there are no sons or daughters, and if the old wife gives him, then only "can that son in-law live with *the new wife* If not so given, he cannot get the "new wife. Neither can that man's presents be received. *She* (the new wife, J.J.) "shall be free from the status of being that man's wife. The reason is that she "was tricked and put to shame. "

S. 133. If the mother gives the daughter in marriage during the absence of the daughter's father, and if the father on his return does not agree to it, he has a right to take that daughter back. In secular affairs (လောကီရေး) the husband alone has the governance of sons and daughters. Even if there be a king's daughter, the husband alone has authority over the wife together with sons and daughters ; therefore it is not right to act in secular affairs without the husband's knowledge. Even if she be a chief queen she has no authority.

Note.—The maxim of the *Menu Kyay*, that the husband is lord of the wife, is judicially recognized by our Courts. The paramount right of the father in preference to the mother in bestoval the daughter is plainly stated in the rules about guardians in s. 28 of Bk 6 of the *Menu Kyay*, as also the father's right to recover the girl from the man to whom the mother gave her without authority from the father. The word which is "lokive " in the Pali edition I have, at Dr. Forchhammer's instance, translated 'secular affairs' as distinguished from spiritual or ecclesiastical affairs. It not the same as "lawka," which means a cycle of entire revolution of nature, something like Plato's year. Even in making religious offerings a wife is to act under her husband's control according to the sections of the *Menu Kyay* quoted in my notes to s. 157 in the next chapter.

S. 134. Persons who from old age are unable to take care of sons or daughters, or grandchildren, or great-grandchildren, or in other words, to give them in marriage, make them over to relatives.

If the relations receive presents and give them in marriage, they have a right to give them in marriage. The real mother and real father must not speak in the matter.

Note.—For the same reason gifts made by old and in becile parents are invalid without consent of the children, as stated in s. 3 of Bk. 8 of the *Menu Kyay* As to children becoming managers when the parents are very old, see the judgment about inheritance in Appendix B.

S. 135. A man gives presents and takes a daughter and goes to a distant place. After fixing a date and giving her maintenance he may go to a distant place. If he goes away to another place without having given her maintenance the mother has a right to take back that daughter. If he gives maintenance, and does not come back for three years, there is a right to a husband and son (*i. e.*, the wife may take another husband and bear a new family). If within three years he dies, and his elder or younger brother comes and wishes to live with her, he may live with her after paying her debts owed to others.

Note.—This subject is discussed under ss. 122 and 131 and in my first note See also ss. 14 to 19 of Bk. 5 of the *Menu Kyay.* The chapter of the *Wonnana* on divorce deals with the subject again.

S. 136. There are four kinds of virgins, namely, a virgin whose sexual desires are similar, a virgin of dissimilar inclination, a virgin of like class and desires, a virgin of like desires but different class.

There are five other kinds, namely, a virgin of similar desirest a virgin of different desires, a virgin of the same class, a virgin no, of the same class, and a virgin slave. Some say that including these five there are nine kinds. A virgin of the class of rulers (ဝင်းချီ) minmyo (the noble class in Dr. Richardson's vocabulary , a virgin of the Brahmin class. a virgin of the trading class, a virgin of the ploughman class (cultivators). In some written decisions it is said that these four kinds, together with the five classified according to the desires, are the nine different kinds.

S. 137. If a man by mutual consent has sexual intercourse with any of the abovementioned virgins he shall not be liable to any damage, but if against the will of the girl he shall be liable to punishment. A man may take a girl of the same class and desires, and if he takes one not of the same class but of the same desires, and then takes another, he shall pay as damage the price of the girl's body. If a man has connection with a minor and thereby spoils her virginity, and if this is done through a go-between it is said by wise men of old that both the man and the go-between, shall have their hair shaved, leaving a cross, and then be taken round the village and beaten with canes and split bamboos, &c. If a man by force spoils a girl and if she thereby dies, he shall pay as damage 10 slaves, but, on the other hand, if the girl consents no damage shall be paid. If a man spoil one of the members of the ruling family, he shall pay 500 tickels of pure silver as damage ; if a member of a Brahmin family, 400 tickels ; if of a merchant's family 300 tickels ; if of a cultivators' family, 200 tickels ; and if of a slave family, 100 tickels. The abovementioned amounts shall be given as damage only when the girl has been made pregnant, otherwise half only of the abovementioned amounts shall be given; but if the co-habitation was done by force the whole amount. A slave virgin means a daughter of a slave by her master, and she is so called because her mother is a slave.

Note.—This and the remaining sections are of less practical importance than the foregoing since the passing of the Indian Penal Code, though valuable as showing the sentiments to which the Burmese law applies. They should be compared with the *Menu Kyay*, Bks. 5 and 6. The classification of virgins begins in s. 27 of Bk. 6; some cases of seduction occur at the beginning of that book. It may here be mentioned that in " Mee Kin *vs.* Nga Myin Gyee," printed in circular memorandum 42 of the 18th October 1882, the Judicial Commissioner ruled that a woman cannot maintain a suit against a paramour on the mere allegation that after consenting to cohabit with him she became pregnant. In a judgment printed in circular memorandum 39 of the 14th October 1882, the Special Court held in a suit for maintenance of children brought by the mother, under the Buddhist law, that as she chose to live separate from her husband and make her own arrangements, she was not entitled to claim maintenance of the children from the father.

S. 138. (*a*). If a man lower in rank than the virgin by force has sexual connection with her against her will, he shall pay as damage all property he possesses, and is also liable to punishment. If, on the other hand, the man be of higher rank, he shall pay as damages 100 tickels of silver. If both are of the same rank, the man shall only be punished, and if the girl consents, they may live as man and wife, but if the man does not wish to take the girl, he shall pay the price of the girl (according to her rank).

(*b*) If a man lower in rank than the virgin has connection with her by force and against her will in a secret place, the forefingers of his left hand shall be cut off, and if he is afraid to allow this being done, he shall pay damage as much as a man of high rank would have to if he did the act. If a man of higher rank did the act, he shall take the girl, and if he does not do so, he shall give all his property. If, on the other hand, he has no property, he shall pay as damage 200 tickels of silver or 600 tickels of copper. If both are of the same rank, and if the man gives a large amount of presents the girl should take him, but if the girl on no account wants the man, he shall pay as damage only 30 tickels of silver, and if she is made pregnant 60 tickels. If before the damage is paid the woman (with child) dies, three times the amount shall be paid. A wise man has said that a man who makes presents and proposes for a virgin and before the consent is given embraces and kisses her, shall pay 15 tickels of silver as damages.

S. 139. Wise men of old have pointed out that if a man has sexual connection with a virgin who is mad or dumb or blind, he shall pay no damage if she consents, but he shall only give her clothing. If he makes her pregnant, he shall give her maintenance and look after her. If the girl dies, he shall pay all funeral expenses as if she were his wife. In other words, if a man has connection with a blind virgin he should take her, and if he does not so wish he shall pay 30 tickels of silver, the value of milk, and he may also be punished and put to shame. If the girl has no parents she alone is entitled to the 30 (tickels), value of milk.

S. 140. If a virgin of high rank makes advances to a man of equal rank, both shall be punished and put to shame by their relatives, and no damages shall be paid. If she consents to a man of higher rank

3

and sexual connection takes place, no damage shall be paid. If she consents to a man of a low rank, she shall be tied and exposed to the sun. Thus it has been said.

S. 141. If after the parents have received presents and betrothed their daughter she is seduced by another man, and if before the presents have been returned, the parents die, the seducer shall return all the presents, for it was he who plucked the girl's flower of virginity.

S. 142. If a virgin go-between seduce a virgin, she shall be made to pay 200 viss of copper. If a woman of mature age acts as the go-between, her hair shall be shaved and she shall be turned out of the country. If the go-between is one of low degree, she shall be made to ride a mule and be taken all round the country, for she did not treat the virgin as her own daughter.

S. 143. If a man obtains a wife by presenting property which does not belong to him, and if the owners of the property come to know about it and take away their property, the parents shall not tell the man that they gave their daughter because they thought the property was his, and that as they have found out the truth they will not give her to him.

S. 144. The following are the 21 kinds of virgins classified by men :—

(1) a virgin of advanced age ;
(2) a minor virgin ;
(3) a diseased virgin ;
(4) a pregnant virgin ;
(5) a virgin come from a distant place ;
(6) a virgin under mother's care ;
(7) a virgin under father's care ;
(8) a virgin under grandmother's care ;
(9) a virgin under elder sister's care ;
(10) a virgin under younger sister's care ;
(11) a virgin under relatives' care ;
(12) a virgin under grandfather's care ;
(13) a virgin under the care of her father's younger brother (သားထွေး။) (this word also means step-father, hence it may mean a virgin under her step-father's care) ;
(14) a virgin under care of her father's elder sister ;
(15) a virgin under the care of her mother's brother ;
(16) a virgin under elder brother's care ;
(17) a virgin under younger brother's care ;
(18) a virgin under the care of her mother's elder sister ;
(19) a virgin under the care of her mother's younger sister (မိထွေး။) (this word also means step-mother, hence it may mean a virgin under the care of her step-mother);
(20) a mad virgin ; and
(21) a virgin under creditor's care.

A daughter who makes herself loved by men, and has a good figure, which makes her look pretty, and has not been spoiled by any man, is called a virgin. A girl of eight years is said to be a "Goyree virgin;" a girl of ten years is said to be a "Konemaree" virgin ; and a girl of 12 years is said to be a **virgin** ; and a girl upwards of that age is said to be a grown-up woman. As long as a woman has had no sexual intercourse with a man, even if she be 60 years old, she is said to be a virgin. If opinion varies from the above sayings of preachers and also about the abovementioned 21 kinds of virgins which is not shown in the *Byar Ga Rine Kyan*, it is left for the person to consider.

Remarks.—The terms *goyree* and *konemaree* are used in the same signification and legal importance in Anglo-Indian law-books, but are spelled " gauri " and " kumari " according to the system of transliteration adopted in Europe and India for all purely Aryan words. No Sanskrit or Pali scholar will be able to identify an Aryan (Pali or Sanskrit) word transliterated according to the system now prevalent in Burma. I spell all Pali words conformant to the Indian and European system of transliteration.

Byargarine kyan is the Pali vyākara*n*am mutilated beyond recognition by the present mode of transliterating Aryan words in Burma. The word has reference to a set of 250 Sanskrit works, which were translated into Burmese by the order of the successor of Alompra a hundred and fifteen years ago : his collection begins which Vopadeva's Sanskrit Grammar (Vyākara*n*am) and is known in Burmese by the technical appellation (ဗျာကရိုက်းစသောတကျုံးတို့) (see *Wonn na* Dhammathat, p. 104), " the books beginning with the Vyākara*n*am, &c." The set contained also the " Samudrika lakshanam " and " Ittishastra," works on palmistry and erotics, from which a good many passages on virgins and women have been abstracted and incorporated in the *M. nu Kyay* and the *Wonn na* in the edition we possess at present. The passage does not occur in the *Wagaru*.

S. 145. (1) a woman taken care of by her mother ;

(2) a woman taken care of by her father ;

(3) a woman taken care of by both her father and mother ;

(4) a woman taken care of by her brother ;

(5) a woman taken care of by her younger sister ;

(6) a woman taken care of by her relations ;

(7) a woman taken care of by her family ;

(8) a woman taken care of by her friend of the same religious habits ;

(9) a woman taken care of by those who promised to look after her when she was yet in the womb ;

(10) a woman taken care of by her lover ;

(11) a woman punished ;

(12) a woman slave bought with and taken by giving property ;

(13) a woman who lives together by mutual consent ;

(14) a woman who lives together for ease and comfort;

(15) a woman who lives together by the mere gift of clothing ;

(16) a woman who lives together because a vow of love has been made by dipping in the water mug ;

(17) a woman who lives together by the removal of the burden *laid on her* in that country ;

(18) a confidential woman slave ;

(19) a woman who lives together *because the man* is a conductor of suits ;

(20) a captive woman ;

(21) a woman who lives together for a short time only ;

if sexual connection takes place with any of the abovementioned 21 kinds of women, *that person* commits a sin.

Out of the abovementioned, the women from the one under the mother's care to the one under the care of the friend of the same religious habits commit no sin *even if sexual connection takes place*, but the men commit sin. Thus it should be noted.

If sexual connection takes place with any of the women from the one taken care of by those who promised to look after her when she was yet in the womb to the one who lives together for a short time only, both the man and the woman commit sin.

The decisions *about* these 21 kinds of women are laid down in the *Tha-man-ta-pa-tha-dee-ka-wence-ah-ta-gee-htar* (သန္တပါသာဒိကဝိနည်း အဋ္ဌကထာ။) and following these they are shown in Dhammathats.

Remarks.—The "Samantapasadika" (Tha-man-ta-pa-tha-deeka) is Budhaghosha's commentary (atthakatha, ah-ta-gee-htar) to the five books of the Vinayapitakam, containing the rules and regulations of the Buddhist priesthood. Budhaghosha lived in the 5th century A D. The "Samantapasadika" and the Visuddhimaggo by the same author, form the chief sources of the purely Buddhistic portion of the Burmese Dhammathats.

DIVORCE.

Translation of the text of the chapter on Divorce in the Manoo Wonnana Dhammathat as edited by Moung Tet Too in Burmese, with Notes by John Jardine, Esq., Bo. C.S., Judicial Commissioner of British Burma, and Remarks by Dr. E. Forchhammer, Professor of Pali.

THERE are seven kinds of wives, *viz.*, a wife like a murderess, a wife like a thief, a wife like a master, a wife like a mother, a wife like a sister, a wife like a friend, and a wife like a slave

Note.—The seven kinds of wives are described in the *Menu Kyay* Dhammathat, Bk. 5, s. 11 ; and again with greater fulness in Bk. 12, s. 1. Both these descriptions are lengthier than those of the *Wannana.* Perhaps these classes are referred to in s. 24 of Bk. 5. In the *Wonnana* one of the wives is that like a murderess ; in the *Menu Kyay* she is compared to an enemy, and her bad dispositions are strikingly portrayed. In our annotations we try to supply for the first time some information about the Hindu and Buddhist sources of the Burman law, and we point out the references to sacred literature. In spite of the close connection of the two codes of marriage, we cannot find that connection at all mentioned in judicial decisions, and as a rule the Burmans are quite ignorant of the Hindu Shasters.

S. 147. A wife who wishes her husband evil, who tries to find fault with him, who through lust loves others besides him, and who does not respect him, is said to be one like a murderess.

S. 148. A wife who hides or squanders the earnings of her husband obtained by cultivating or trading is said to be one like a thief.

S. 149. An idle wife, who does not look after the house, who is a glutton, who is rude in her ways and vulgar in her conversation, who complains and ill-treats a persevering husband, is said to be one like a master.

S 150. A wife who looks after the welfare of her husband as a mother looks after her child, who keeps him away from all harm and evil, and who makes good use of the property, is said to be one like a mother.

Note.—For a view of the Burman's notions of wifely duty see the more embellished descriptions in the *Manu Kyay*, Book 12, of which the following is a sample :—

" A wife like a mother is this : a mother, from the time her child is conceived and born till he arrives at puberty, takes care that no bugs, gnats, mosquitoes, or horseflies shall bite him. If he be in the charge of any other person, she fears they will hurt him or give him improper food, that they do not love him as she does, that they may both love and hate him at the same time. If he cries of his own accord, she thinks some one has beaten him : if others give him the best of food, she thinks there may be poison in it, and only wishes him to eat what she herself prepares for him ; is contented if he be asleep or idle, and be he dressed as he may, thinking him handsome, she is happy ; when he sleeps she will not leave him till he awakes, lest anything bad befall him ; if he goes in the sun or the rain, she is anxious about him, and fears lest he should fall ; though she herself has neither rest nor food, if her child has, she is satisfied, wishes to hear his happy voice, thinks even his abuse and bad language pleasant, but quietly kisses and gently checks him, saying "these are bad words, do not repeat them my son," and out of the hearing of others constantly advises him in all matters as to the way it is proper or not proper to go, the proper time for coming, the proper time for remaining, the proper time for sleeping, the proper time for eating ; advises him to avoid the five sins of killing, stealing. adultery, lying, and drinking, and constantly instructs him that the images, the laws, and priests, the three gems, are the proper objects of worship ; places him with a good teacher, and if he praise him she is delighted ; wishes him to be a priest ; or if he remain as a (lay) man, wishes him to take a wife from an excellent family, and wishes to the end of her life to attend on him. In infancy, when she takes him to her bosom, he pulls her hair, kicks and scratches her face and breast, bites and scratches her lips, and though he relieve his natural wants on her, she is not disgusted. In this way, as a woman loves her child, so a wife (who reflects) that this is the husband given her by her parents, or the husband got by the instrumentality of a go-between, or that he is the husband of her choice and she the wife of his, and eats not unless he eats, and sleeps not unless he sleeps, that he is a man, and manhood is a gift from God which a woman must use greater endeavours before she can obtain ; thinks him comely in eating or in dress, wishes to dress and ornament him that he may surpass others in the assembly, and wishes to know the reasons of his going out ; expects and looks out for him in his return ; wishes to give him his clothes (to dress) and prepare his meals for him ; and though he may go after other women let not others know it. but concealing the fact, advises him in bed, when no one is present (a curtain lecture) : a wife who thus consults the wishes of her husband and acts in this way, and has good sentiments, is a wife like a mother, and such a wife ought to be loved.

S. 151. A wife who respects her husband as a young sister respects her elder brother, who feels ashamed and is afraid of him as a sister of her brother, and who gives in to him in all that he does, is said to be one like a sister.

S. 152. A wife who tries to make her husband happy, as a man rejoices to see the arrival of his friend from a far country, who is of an upright mind, and who knows her duty towards her husband. is said to be one like a friend.

S. 153. A wife who has a quiet disposition, who remains quiet even when struck or punished, who by kind words makes her husband turn away from evil to good, is said to be one like a slave.

Note.—In s 46 of Bt. 12 of the *Menu Kyay* the submissive conduct of a wife is highly praised. The sacred law is quoted against itself as applauding even the wife of a hunter who hands him quiver, bow, and arrows and receives the prey from his hands. She is to be saved from hell and receive advantage from her dutiful conduct ; while the hunter himself is foredoomed to dreadful hills because he takes animal life.

Remarks—The passage treating of the seven kinds of wives is a discourse ascribed to Yasôdhara, the wife of Gautama. before he became a Buddha. I give the whole passage as contained in the Sinhalese *Singalovadasiutta sanne* (Hardy, Man. of Buddhism, p. 483). The Pali text is taken from the *Suttapitakam* and therefore belongs to the sacred Buddhist canon, In the discourse delivered by Yasôdhara dewi, in the presence of men, dewas, and Brahmas. immediately previous to her death, she described the seven kinds of wives, that there are in the world of men :—

1. *Wadhaka, the executioner.*—This woman always thinks ill of her husband, though protesting continually that she loves him ; she associates with other men and flatters them. If her husband be a poor man, she asks him for something it is not in his power to give her, and then reproaches him because he does not receive it ; and she sits on a higher seat in his presence.. Though such a woman should have a person beautiful as that of a dewi, be of a respectable family, and possess many slaves, she is not the wife of her husband ; she is like a manacle tightly fastened by the executioner, or an iron collar encircling his neck, or a weapon always prepared to wound him, or a sword so sharp that it will cut a hair.

2. *Chori, the thief*—This woman is seldom in the house of her husband, but goes to the market-place, or the field, or wherever there is a multitude of people ; she is acquainted with many ways of sin ; she hides whatever property is brought into the house by her husband,—hides it from him, but reveals it to other man ; she tells abroad his secrets ; she appears to despise any ornaments and other things that he gives her, and asks pettishly for what he does n t give ; she shows no kindness to her husband's relatives or friends ; she shuns the company of the good and associates with the bad. She is not like his wife, but like an ulcer on his body or a cancer, or an incurable disease ; she is like a fire in a dry forest, or an axe for cutting down the tree of merit.

3. *Swami, the ruler.*—This woman does not in any way strive to benefit her husband, but to injure him ; she leaves the house and runs hither and thither, she lets the work of the house remain undone ; her mind goes out after other men ; she is continually eating ; she hankers after things that do not belong to her station ; she proclaims her own fame and gives no credit to others ; she despises her husband and rules him as if he was her slave, and is like a messenger sent from Yama to frighten him.

These three descriptions of women when they die will be tormented in hell, therefore their ways are to be avoided.

4 *Matu, the mother.*—This woman loves her husband as a mother, takes care of his property, provides his meals at the proper time, and is always anxious for his prosperity, when he does anything wrong she affectionately reproves him and threatens to return to her own relatives if he will not do that which is right ; she gives him good advice and recommends him to be industrious, loyal, and to go and hear bana. She is like a divine medicine for the curing of all diseases, or a branch of the kalpa-tree that gives whatever is requested from it.

5. *Bhagini, the sister.*—The woman pays the same reverence to her husband that a sister does to her brother ; she gives him all that is in the house ; she wishes that he may receive whatever she sees others possess ; and she loves him alone and no other man.

6. *Sakhi, the faithful friend.*—This woman is always thinking about her husband when he is absent and looks out continually for his return ; it gives her pleasure to hear of him, and when he returns she is delighted to see him ; she associates with his friends and not with his enemies ; his friends are her friends and his enemies are her enemies ; she hides his faults and proclaims aloud his goodness ; she stops those who are abusing him and encourages those who praise ; she tells others of his virtues and greatness ; she keeps no secrets from him and does not reveal those with which he entrusts her ; she is sorry when any misfortune happens to him and rejoices in his prosperity ; and she provides for him the best food.

7. *Dasi, the slave.*—This woman does not resent the abuse of her husband, however brutal it may be ; she does all that is required of her with alacrity ; she keeps at the utmost distance from all improper conduct with other men ; she first gives food that has been nicely prepared to her husband, or any guest there may be in the house, and then eats herself ; she retires to rest after her husband and is up before he rises ; she is economical in her expenditure, she commends and exalts her husband, but is herself lowly as a slave ; and is like a helper in the procuring of merit, or a shield in warding off demerit.

According to the institutes of Vishnu (Vishnu Smriti) the duties of a wife are as follows :—

(1) Now the duties of a woman are as follows) :—
(2) to live in harmony with her husband ;
(3) to show reverence (by embracing their feet and such like attentions) to her mother-in-law, father-in-law, to gurus such as elders', to divinities, and to guests ;
(4) to keep household articles (such as the winnowing basket and the rest) in good array
(5) to maintain saving habits ;
(6) to he careful with her (pestle and mortar and other) domestic utensils;
(7) not to practice incantations with roots (or other kinds of witches);
(8) to observe auspicious customs ;
(9) not to decorate herself with ornaments (or to partake of amusements) while her husband is absent from home ;
(10) not to resort to the houses of strangers (during the absence of her husband) ;

(11) not to stand near the doorway or by the windows (of her house);

(12) not to act by herself in any matter;

(13) to remain subject, in her infancy to her father, in her youth to her husband, and in her old age to her sons;

(14) after the death of her husband to preserve her chastity, or to ascend the pile after him;

(15) no sacrifice, no penance, and no fasting is allowed to women apart from their husbands; to pay obedience to her lord is the only means for a woman to obtain bliss in heaven;

(16) a woman who keeps a fast or performs a penance in the lifetime of her lord deprives her husband of his life and will go to hell;

(17) a good wife, who peserveres in a chaste life after the death of her lord will go to heaven like (perpetual) students, even though she has no son.

S. 154. Out of these the first three kinds of wives may be divorced (ஞ்கွ)   kwa) even if they have had ten children, but the other four kind   sould not even until death be divorced.

Note.—The parallel passages in the *Menu Kyay* are the following:—

Book 5, s. 11. Amongst these seven kinds of wives, the wife like a mother, the wife like a sister, the wife like a friend, and the wife like a slave ought not to be put away by any man, but should be lived with for life. The wife like a master, the wife like an enemy, the wife like a thief, these three, even if they have borne ten children may he put away; they need not be lived with for one day, and of the seven, the wife like a slave, if she pray to be a man in the next life, will not be disappointed; her prayer will be fulfilled and before others she will obtain neik-ban. Thus the gods Pitsay ka Bandoh have praised them. Thus the Yathay called menu said.

Bk 12, s. 2. Of these seven kinds of wives, the wife like an enemy, the wife like a thief, wise men of the law, if it be proved after careful examination that they are so, have the power to give judgment as in the case of an enemy or a thief.

Some need for impartial decision would arise from the permission given in s. 45 of Bk. 12 to the husband to sell the wife who took a paramour. The husband could not be judge of his own cause, and a judicial procedure is described in s. 36 of Bk. 6, which must be compared with the provisions about paramours in s. 3 of Bk. 12. Trials by ordeal were also sanctioned as in the Mosaic and Hindu Codes, the Burmese ordeals were by fire, water, chewing rice, and by molten lead,—*see* s. 680, &c., of the *Wounana* and Bk. 9, s. 16 of the *Menu Kyay* If the violator were of exalted rank he might find a substitute or purge himself by mere oath in certain cases; *see* ss. 34 and 35 of Bk. 6. The giving of property to paramours and lesser wives is discussed in Bk. 8, s. 3, pp. 236 and 239 of Richardson's edition. These rules are worthy of attention as showing the policy of the law to be opposed to immorality. The power of the wife to give away property is limited as the following extract shows :—

" In case of the wife making a gift without the knowledge of her husband, whether it be to her paramour or not, she has no right to confer a gift unknown to her husband; if the husband shall take it back, let him have it. This is only said of things equally the property of both. In case they shall both have been married before, if the wife, without the knowledge of the husband, shall confer a gift of part of the property on any person other than her paramour, let her have the right to do so, the husband cannot claim it back, let him only correct his wife for not having told him. Even if the thing given be part of the property brought with her, if she confer a gift on a paramour, or a person of whom the husband has suspicion (under the idea) that she has right to her original property, she has no right to do so without the knowledge of her husband; let him have the right to take back the whole." The rules in s. 108 of the Indian Contract Act must also be considered in such matters.

S. 155. A woman who possesses good qualities is said to be a loving wife. The woman who loves her husband is a wife that should be retained and should not be divorced, even if liable to illness.

Note.—The Burmese Dhammathats contain the doctrine of the Hindu lawyers as to the penal character of desertion. The following among other texts collected in Colebrooke's Digest prove the identity :—

Nareda.—A husband who abandons an affectionate wife, or her who speaks not harshly, who is sensible, constant, and fruitful, shall be brought to his duty by the King with a severe chastisement.

Vishnu.—A man who deserts a faultless wife shall suffer the same punishment

Devala—No atonement is ordained for that man who forsakes his own wife through delusion of mind, deserting her illegally, nor for him who forsakes a virtuous son.

Manu.—She who, though afflicted with illness, is beloved and virtuous, must never be disgraced, though she may be superseded by another wife with her own consent.

The husband was also liable to a penalty of a third part of his property : for the reference see Note to s. 170.

This section 155 is also supported by ss. 173 and 176 to 178. It appears to me a correct statement of the general rule of Buddhist law as displayed in the Dhammathats. As might be expected, the law coincides with the established notions of morals. The exceptions stated in other sections make the rule clearer. The passage in s. 3 of Bk 12 of the *Manu Kyay* about the *Kan* or *Karma* or balance of merits in past existences, which is the basis of the doctrine of *ex-parte* divorce applied by the Recorder of Rangoon in so many cases, and which is the passage usually quoted in support of that doctrine by Burmans, has received the learned attention of Dr. Forchhammer since I wrote my second Note on marriage. The similar language of s. 43 of Bk 12 and s. 54 of Bk. 10, may be noticed. On a matter about which the only opinion of value must be that of a scholar I need say no more : but I would especially draw the attention of the Burmans (who are in my experience generally unable to explain the literary allusions of the Dhammathats and completely ignorant of their connections with Indian law) to the introductory remarks of my learned friend. Even in getting the real sense of the Burmese edition, more than a superficial knowledge of the Burmese language is wanted. The Burman language usually conveys two ideas : one of mere abandonment or desertion, which is pronounced to be illegal, and is an act of ill-temper or wickedness ; the other is divorce which, unless effected by mutual consent, required formality and impartial investigation. Moung Htine states a distinction never mentioned to me by any European, or any other Burman, though probably known to Dr. Richardson Where the word *kwa* (divorce is used by itself a separation by mutual consent is implied : where two verbs are used, namely, *sun kwa* (abandon) (separate) the meaning is, he says, a separation or abandonment caused by the act of one party only I hope some student of Páli will remember this when the Páli edition is translated as the Recorder's interpretation of these antique laws affects the whole law of marriage and inheritance.

Remarks.—Kwa (ကွာ) in Burmese is an intransitive verb. *khwa* (ခွါ) the corresponding transitive form ; the former implies that the act of breaking takes place without any direct external agency hence in a legal sense by " mutual consent " Khwa indicates that the act of breaking is caused by an external agent, by a third party, not the two concerned in the breaking. See *Menu Kyay,* page 357 § 44, " though she and her husband do not wish to separate, but to live together, if the " parents of the woman wish to separate them, they shall have the power." Their mutual consent not to separate is expressed by (ကွာပြင်မဆို॥) where *kwa* alone used confirming the sagacious remark of Moung Htine. The power of the parents (as a third party) to separate them against their mutual consent is expressed by the causative or transitive form of the verb, namely, *Khwa* (ခွါ) (ဖိအစွန့်ခွါကာ). *Sun* means ' to give up." to abandon *ex-parte,* because the antithetic verb *tun* implies " to do something by joint contribution." Moung Htine is therefore correct in maintaining that *sun kwa* means separation or abandonment by one party only.[+]

In Páli the verb *chaddeti* (is generally used to convey the forcible putting away (of a wife), and is in Burmese rendered by the more emphatic (စွန့်ပြစ်တာ၊ရှင်း)॥ *cajjati,* the passive of *cajahati* (to abandon, to give up is used for Burmese *sun kwa;* also *jahati* and *vijahati* ; but the Páli is not capable of expressing the fine distinctions of the Burmese *sun, kwa, khwa,* or *sun kwa,* in the verbs themselves.

S. 155. A woman who is barren. a woman who always brings forth female children, also a woman who has bodily deficiencies, a woman who bears neither daughters nor sons, a woman with leprosy, a woman of bad conduct, a woman who has no love for her husband, or in other words, a woman who having no love for her husband has a paramour, these five kinds of wives may be abandoned or divorced (*Sun pyit Kwa Shin*).

Note.—In paragraph 32 of may second Note the reader will find the reasons given by the Pāli Professor, Dr. Forchhammer, for considering this section to be the nucleus of the Burman law about divorce.

Ss. 156 and 176 must be considered together when we compare them with the Hindu texts cited by Colebrooke. For certain matters, such as the Hindu law treats as reasons for excluding from inheritance, either husband or wife might refuse conjugal rights to the other, and the wife might in other ways be superseded. I refer to leprosy, elephantiasis, marasmus, and genital diseases Moung Kyaw Doon alone among the Europeans and Burmans whom I consulted explained in this sense the passage interpreted as an authority for the doctrine of free *ex-parte* divorce :—"When there is no fault on either side but their destinies are not cast together." This is in s. 3 of Bk. 12 of the *Menu Kyay*: in s. 43 the same expression is distinctly used regarding these diseases. Dr. Forchhammer comes to the same opinion as Moung Kyaw Doon, who could not give his reason at all clearly, but supplied me with the hint in paragraph 38 of may second Note. The bodily diseases and certain immoralities are set forth in the Hindu books very much as in the Burmese codes: compare Colebrooke on the duties of a husband and exclusion from inheritance. The clear doctrine is that loathsome disease results from sin which may have been committed in a former existence. The wife so afflicted may be refused conjugal rights, and, as Devala puts it, he excluded from business, or, according to manu and Cullucabhatta, another wife may be taken ; but as shown by the following texts she could not be divorced, and apparently could not abandon the husband unless he repudiated her.

Yajnyawakya.—A superseded wife, must be maintained : else a great offence is committed.

Manu.—If a wife, legally superseded, shall depart in wrath from the house she must either instantly be confined or abandoned in the presence of the whole family.

As to ill-tokens discovered by palmistry, redundant fingers, and other concealed blemishes in a betrothed girl, see the Hindu texts 183 to 185 in Bk. 4, Chap. 4 of Colebrook's Digest.

The above five causes are similar to those mentioned in the ancient Hindu law books as entitling a husband to supersude his first wife by taking another, not to divorce her, divorce being contrary to the sacramental ideas of the Hindu law. The Buddhist law as stated in the *Menu Kyay* coincides with the Hindu law, e. g., Bk. 5, s. 18, as regards leprous and diseased wives—"Let the husband "minister to her in the most proper manner ; he has a right to cease connubial con- "nection with her. He shall have no right to put her away (sun) with her pro- " perty. If he takes a lesser wife he has a right to do so."

Book 12, s. 43, refers to all the five sorts of women, and the writer imme- diately explains that only supersession is intended by adding a proviso :—"By putting away (sun) is not meant that he may take all the property and put her away, but if he wishes he may take another wife, and a wife as above shall have no right to oppose his wishes ; thus she may be said to be put away (sun). This is one point in the matter." If he had been induced to marry a leprous or deformed woman without knowing of the defect, he could, under s. 128 of the *Wonnana* recover the presents from the girl's parents and so be in a pecuniary position to contract for some one else.

If the bad conduct degenerated into adultery, the husband was entitled to divorce as stated in the end of s. 43 of Bk. 12 of the *Menu Kyay*. As explained under ss. 154 and 175, I mean a divorce after judicial inquiry, where the woman denied the charge. It is of vast importance to note the difference beween the two propositions :—(1) a husband for valid cause may divorce his wife ; (2) a husband on a valid cause of action may apply to a Court for a decree of divorce against his wife. Strange to say the distinction is unknown to many Englishmen in Burma ;

and although every one of the Burmese Judges whom I have consulted say deliberately on second thought that no mere abandonment whatever has validity as divorce without mutual consent, unless so decreed by a competent Court, it has always appeared to me that the point was not present to their minds although seen clearly enough when I put the following questions:—Has a jealous or angry husband or wife lawful power to dissolve the status of marriage by his or her own will? If the one refuses to accept the fiat of the other, or to have any a ward of arbitrators how can the status be dissolved?

The *Shwe Myee-i*, the **Manoo Reng**, and the *Vagara* Dhammathats contain the same rule as s. 156 of the *Wonnana*. It is more fully discussed in paragraphs 30 to 32 of my second Note on marriage.

S. 157. Wise men have said that the following are the six faults for which a woman may be beaten but not divorced (mahsun mah kwa). A woman who is fond of liquor, one who does not lock after household affairs, one who is in the habit of scolding her husband, one who is fond of gadding about, one who is in the habit of making acquaintance and mixing with men besides her husband, and one who always sits at the doorway of the house. In olden books the Pali word " sapuma " was translated as a woman who kept a lesser husband (paramour ?), but this should not be the translation in the section.

Note.—This last remark is connected with the matter discussed in paragraph 32 of my second Note.

Remarks.—*Sapumo* means literally " with (a) man,' but it depends on the context, in what sense it is to be taken. The *Manoo Reng* Dhammathat (para-12) differs in the Pali text considerably from the *Wonnana* Dhammathat ; it disjoins " Sapumā " from its connection, and translates it ယောက်ျားတယောက်ရှိ ယောဝိန်းမလည်းတံယောက်။ a woman who has (another) man, and then continues with " sāmivādanam," which is rendered a (woman) who seeks to quarrel with her husband. The *Wonnana* and *Wagaru* are *more* correct in the Pali text and Burmese translation. *Wonnana* Dhammathat : Sāminan ca vivādana ; vivādana is the correct word (not *vadanam*, as in the *Manoo Reng*), implying the idea of dissenting words, quarrel, as opposed to samavādanum, words of reconciliation ; and then the *Wonnana* continues : Gathasilava Sapuma, a woman who is in the habit of making acquaintance with other men. The *Wagaru* and *Manoo Sara* coincide with the *Wonnaua*. I have already pointed out that the *Manoo Reng* commits in the paragraph preceding the one under comment another serious blunder in selecting the word *sappuriso* for *sapumo* and translating it " a good man," instead of with (her) male (husband), sapume na icchanti, not desiring (to stay with) her husband. The compiler of the *Wonnana* evidently corrects the blunders of the *Manoo Reng.*

Note —The editor of the *Manoo Wonnana* having described the contract of marriage in one chapter has already described the duties of the wife according to the moral law to which, as we have seen, the religious sanction of the Buddhist doctrine of future lives is attached, especially in the *Menu Kyay.* He then states the principle that a virtuous woman is not to be divorced, and next he specifies the five ordinary causes of divorce. Having done this he treats of incompatible habits and domestic irritations for which the husband, who is lord of the wife, may chastise her but which, unless and until they prove incorrigible. are not at all sufficient reasons for dissolution of the marriage bond. This logical arrangement helps us to perceive how exactly the jurist is in accord with the sustained doctrine of Judges in England. Light or hasty resort to the remedy by divorce is not allowed, marriage being a social institution as well as a private contract. As in England, the husband is held to be the guardian of his wife's honour ; and he is enjoined to use goodness and discretion to secure his conjugal comfort, and where these means fail he is armed with the same power of chastising as the old common law allowed in England and similar to but not so great as that conceded to parents in s. 47 of Bk. 12 of the *Menu Kyay.* (See also s. 632 of the *Wonnana.*) In Bk. 5, s. 12 of the *Menu Kyay* the language, except as regards the Hindu suspicion of women, is not unlike a judgment of the Judge Ordinary. "Any woman may have six faults. These six faults are, drinking intoxicating liquors keeping bad company, paying no attention to her husband's requests, who disputes his wishes, eating before her husband is satisfied; having unlawful habits, keeping a paramour, gadding about from one house to another. These are the six, faults, and a woman being free from them should in the most proper way minister to her husband. Few women are satisfied with one husband, nor are they careful of the honour of their family. When out of sight, they do not consider what is good and what is bad ; their desires are changeable and unfixed ; they have all a desire for all they see. With women who have these bad habits, a man should be much on his guard, and advise them that they should not associate with improper people, nor do any (improper) unlawful acts, have a paramour, nor gad about to other people's houses, nor use improper language. Thus if a man who is wise and capable of reflection shall correct his wife, she will not dispute his authority, but will behave herself with the greatest propriety ; and as they follow the advice of a husband, it is proper that he should advise or correct them. It is not proper to give women their own way. Thus the Lord Recluse called Menu, the son of the King of Bymas said."

The sentiment of this passage is decidedly Hindu. Manu quotes the Vedas against women, and the same language is found in the great Hindu epics quoted by Colberooke. A woman is to be constantly under guardianship.

Manu.—Drinking spirituous liquor, associating with evil persons, absence from her husband, rambling abroad, unseasonable sleep, and dwelling in the house of another are six faults which bring infamy on a married woman.

Vyasa.—Sitting at the door, continually looking out from the windows, conversing with despicable persons, and laughing unseasonably are faults which bring infamy on the women of a family.

Yajnyawalkya.—A woman whose husband resides abroad must avoid sports personal decoration, crowds and jubilees, laughter and visits to the house of strangers.

The Hindu writings contain many other instances of misbehaviour ; and the husband is authorised to inflict different sorts of penances and mild beatings. The Burman rules do not greatly vary from the summary in the *Mitakshara.* " Wives, if unchaste, should be expelled, and so may those who are perverse. But the latter must be supported, provided they be not unchaste. For a maintenance must not be refused solely on account of perverseness."

Colebrooke also points out that the Hindu law treats the litigation of teachers and husbands and the rest as not laudable other in a moral or civil view : therefore pupils, wives, and the rest should, in the first instance, be discouraged by the King or the Court. The same ideas distinctly pervade the Burmese codes. The husband is encouraged to use repeated corrections to enforce those duties which the law bases on morality and religion in the first instance : in the last resort there may be recourse to the tribunal which is required in express words to dissuade the couple from separating, as shown in s. 177 below and in s. 54 of the *Wini Tsaya Paka Thani.* This procedure is adopted to one of the judgments in appendix. As in India there was no redress against the husband except by application to the tribunal, the wife not being armed with power to chastise. But undue resort to the King to enforce moral obligations was in both India and Burma prevented by the power given to the King to fine and otherwise punish immorality or caprice, and by the confiscation of property, even of stridhan in India and payin in Burman.

In the 12th Bk. of the *Menu Kyay,* s. 42, the rule is stated as follows :— " A man shall not put away a wife for one or all of these habits, but as it is laid down above (in the case of five other improprieties described in s. 42 as such as do not by themselves entitle the husband to separation : also described in s. 158 below) let him correct her three times. If he continue to live with her, if he cannot master her, and she continue her former habits, let the decision be the same as above : let the law in both cases be the same." In Bk. 5, s. 24, openly obscene behaviour is treated as entitling to a divorce ; in Bk. 12, at the end of s. 43, the woman's adultery is so treated as we have seen already. The writer of the 5th Bk. in the following sections calls into play the very strongest sanctions of the Buddhist religion to induce husbands and wives to live together sober, righteous, and pious lives, and whether from ignorance or design attributes the injunctions to the mythical Hindu law-giver Manu as in the quotation about the seven wives, although the origin is religious and Buddhistic.

S. 20. When the husband's habits are those of an excellent man, the wife should follow his example and adopt the same habits. If the wife's habits are those of an excellent person, the husband should follow her example and adopt the same habits. If the same habits are corresponding, the goodness of the husband is the happiness of the wife, and the goodness of the wife the happiness of the husband ; for this reason any such husband and wife are said to be people from the country of the Nats and Bymas. If the husband's habits are good and the wife will not follow, or the wife's habits are good and the husband will not follow, the party whose habits are good may think the one who will not follow a person from hell or the region of Pyeitas.

S. 21. If any husband and wife are of equal birth and family, and if on the strength of this the wife make religious offerings without the husband's knowledge, she has no right to do so ; and if she does so, the advantage (merit) which she ought to obtain will not be much. Religious offerings should be made with the knowledge of the husband, and if so made, she obtains the merit of love and respect for her husband, and that of her faith. If the husband makes religious offerings without the knowledge of his wife, or offerings of affection to other people, he has a right to do so ; and the wife * also obtains merit. The wife has no right to object to offerings of the husband, but he may object to those of the wife. This is because the husband is the lord of the wife. It is a work of excellence when both equally, and with faith, make religious offerings or gifts of affection. If neither party habitually perform their religious duties, and are equally negligent in making religious offerings, they have come from the condition, in a previous life, of a male and female brute, and they shall at death go to hell, the condition of a pyeita, an athoorakay, or a brute, the four states to be avoided. Thus the Lord Recluse called Menu said.

Remarks.—These two passages are taken from the Anzurasutta of the Suttapateeya, the III section of the Dighanikayo, which is the first of the five books of the Suttapitakam, which contains the discourses of Gaudama to the laity, and forms the second great division of the Buddhist sacred canon.

S. 158. The following are the five kinds of misconduct for which a wife may be chastised but not divorced (mah kwa mah sun) :

Misconduct with regard to property, with regard to dress and ornaments, with regard to food, with regard to glances of the eye, and with regard to behaviour towards men.

Note.—These five habits in some particular points come under the six categories of the last section. In s. 42 of Bk. 12 of the *Menu Ky y* they are entitled " the five faults for the commission of which only a wife shall not be abandoned." That section is well worth reading, as it throws a bright light on the standard of manners The variety of specification reveals the anxiety of the writer to prevent an angry, passionate Burman from abandoning his wife in mere ill-temper, The relief given is stated in the following words (page 353 of Richardson) :—

" A man may not put away (sun) a wife who is guilty of any or all of these improprieties ; he has a right to chastise her with a bullock-driver's wand or split bamboo on the lions, posteriors, or feet. If after one, two, or three chastisements she quietly lays aside her bad habits and lives correctly, it is not proper to separate from her. If they do separate, it shall only be permitted on the husband giving

* *Note by Dr. Richardson.*—In the Tavoy copy the " wife " is not said to get merit.

her all she is entitled to. If after frequent correction she still continues her bad habits, let each take the property they had in possession at the time of marriage, let the husband take all the property acquired by both during the time of their living together, and let him put her away. If they have no property, he shall not take her price ; he shall only have the right to divorce her (sun). If her habits are those above detailed, and she wish to separate contrary to the inclination of her husband, let him take all their mutual property, and let the wife pay him also her price ; so it is written. One-half of her price is also laid down. If there be any debts, let her alone bear them. Thus the Sage Recluse said."

Remarks.—A wife according to Manu (VIII, 299, 300) may be corrected when she commits faults "with a rope or small short cane ; but on the back part only of the body and not on a noble part by any means."

S. 159. Misconduct with regard to property is when *a woman* keeps property outside which should be kept inside, and keeps property inside which should be kept outside, and without the knowledge of the husband takes, hides, or buys and sells, or pays away debts and takes what is due.

S 160. Misconduct with regard to ornaments is when *a woman* puts on ornaments without taking into consideration time or place, and by day or night uses them, when at home or in the jungle, when at poays, teasts (ပွဲလာ), or funeral house (အဝရှလာ).

Note.—In the *Menu Kyay* women are solemnly enjoined to wear only the dress of their own class.

S 161. Misconduct with regard to food is when *a woman* eats before the husband, when *she* eats with him and goes away before him, and then returns and eats with others, when *she* before the time eats often, when *she* secretly buys and eats in order that her husband may not know, and when *she* gives her husband a little and takes a great quantity herself.

S. 162. Misconduct with regard to glances of the eyes is when *a woman* looks like a crow at any men *she* sees, turning her eyes in all directions.

S. 163. Misconduct with regard to behaviour towards man is when *a woman* laughs and talks with others and behaves with them like as *she* does towards her husband.

S. 164. Pride of beauty, pride of lineage, pride of relatives, and pride of property. Women who possess these four kinds of pride should not be divorced (mah sun mah kwa'.

Note.—This subject is more fully discussed in the *Menu Kyay*, Bk. 12, s. 47. If after three corrections the wife is incorrigible there may be a separation, and the rule for partition is laid down.

S. 165. Thus a daughter already given in marriage, whether *she* lives together or eats and lives in a separate house, goes and lives with her mother and father. If the said husband does not return within three years, and if he does not give or send anything for eating and expenses, after the expiration of that *third* year she has a right to take a husband. If for three years, let her wait. If he is gone to the battle-field, let her wait for six years. If he is gone in search of property, let her wait for seven years. If he is gone in pursuit of charitable and good deeds, let her wait for eight years. If he is gone in search of learning, let her wait for ten years only. If before the above mentioned days and dates and within the month and year she takes a husband, she has not that right. If those periods have expired, she can take a husband and get a son. If the original husband returns, she shall only be handed over. It within the period already mentioned, though it be month or year, if the wife spends, only that taken in possession can be got ; the reason is because he has not the right to say "this is my property."

Note.—This wife's right to re-marry because of the husband's absence and neglect is fully discussed in my commentary on s. 122 in the chapter on marriage. In s. 135 it is supposed that the absent husband has fixed a date for his return. (See also s 131.) With slight variations the respective periods of absence are those mentioned by Devala, Manu, and Vasishtha. Texts 152, &c., of Colebrooke.

S. 166. If a woman's husband is taken captive and the wife takes another husband, then when peace prevails in the country and the former husband returns that wife should be handed over and the presents shall be forfeited The reason is because the woman did not wait and because knowingly *the man* took her. If for long months and years *he does not return, the wife* shall not be given over to him.

S. 167. A husband through anger abandons his wife and, without leaving or giving any maintenance, goes to a distant place. The wife through poverty borrows money *to support herself*, and the creditor takes *the woman* to the knowing and seeing of the people. If afterwards the former husband arrives, he shall not speak. If that former husband loves his wife, he can take her after paying the debts. If he does not pay up the debts, he cannot take ; thus it should be pointed out.

Note.—See ss. 14, 15, and 16 of Bk. 5 of the *Menu Kyay.*

S. 168. If a man wishes to go to a distant place, *he* should give maintenance and then go. If he goes away without leaving any, the expiration of eight years should be waited for, and if beyond that period, *the wife* has a right to take a husband. If because the real (former) husband returns the wife is given over, and *he* says "I do not want her," that wife has the right to take all the original property (payin) which that original husband brought. If *he* has no original property, the price of the body (30 tickels) should be given. The wife should wait for three years, but if she does not wait and the former husband returns and *she* is given back to him and *she* says "I do not want him," the former husband shall take all the property and enquire as to the amount of the presents previously received, and after taking all the original presents given *he,* should turn her out of the house.

Note.—According to Hindu Manu the husband ought to settle the maintenance before starting as in this section and in the *Menu Kyay,* Bk. 5. Both codes enjoin the woman to live circumspectly and work for her living.

S. 169. After a long while *the wife*, impelled by her sexual desires, takes a new husband after telling the loogyees and thoogyees of the village. This husband, in the same manner, goes away, and the wife in the same manner takes another husband, who likewise goes away. If after the absence of the first husband for nine years, the next husband for six years, and the last husband for three years all the three return together, which of them is the man entitled to get that wife? *The reply is* the last husband alone is the one entitled to get, and not the others. Thus it should be pointed out.

S. 170. If either a husband or a wife desires to divorce, let the person who is (နိဿယ) naithaya (supporter) obtain two-thirds and the person who is (နိဿိတ) naitheeta (dependent) one-third of the property, and let them in the same manner get the debts due and owing to them. So be it. As regards debt-property, the texts are contradictory and opinions are divided. A wife is said to be the (နိဿယ) naithaya (supporter) and her husband (နိဿိတ) naitheeta (dependent) when the wife at the time of the marriage possesses large property which may increase by being used as principal in trade (yinhnee yingwai), or when the husband is wholly dependent upon his wife's exertion for his living, and a husband is said to be supporter and his wife dependent when the case is the contrary.

If such husband and wife wish to divorce by mutual consent let the supporter obtain two-thirds and the dependent one-third of the property consisting of animate and inanimate in possession. As for the debts they owe, the supporter shall pay one-third and the dependent two-thirds, because it is to be understood that the supporter laboured and had anxiety and trouble from the time such debts were contracted and the supporter worked for gain while the dependent did not labour and lived eating and sleeping. As for the property in possession they shall get one-third or two-thirds in proportion to their status.

When the husband and wife are sharers of each other's proverty and prosperity and are helpmates to each other let the property be divided equally, and in the case of either party possessing some property originally (ပါရင်း) (payin let the owner get it. If the said property is spent or lavished, there can be no compensation. The husband gets the sons and the wife the daughters, who are children begotten by both. There is no offence committed if the husband sells the sons he gets, but if he sells the daughters he shall make good half (of the proceeds of sale), and a similar compensation shall be given by the wife if she sells the sons.

Note —This and the following section are discussed in paragraph 42 of my second Note on marriage, which contains a full commentary on the section of the *Manu Kyay* about partition.

The following Hindu texts regarding the find of property may be quoted here from Colebrooke :—

Yajnyawalkya —He who forsakes a wife though obedient to his commands, diligent in household management, mother of an excellent son, and speaking kindly, shall be compelled to pay the third part of his wealth : or, if poor, to provide a maintenance for that wife.

Nareda.—The man who abandons an unblemished damsel after accepting her shall be amerced in a pecuniary fine : and he must marry that damsel.

Remarks —ဣုက္ကဒ္ဓန် တထေဝစဉ့် စကားကိုပြု၍ဖြစ်၍ အယူပြားကြ၏။ This passage is inserted by the author (or compiler) of the *Wonnana* : he means : as regards debt-property "(inaudhanam), the texts (of the Dhammathats) are contradictory (or corrupted) and opinions are divided (as to the proper meaning of the passage)."

S. 171. If a husband or wife in a state of angers says to the other " I do not love you," such words shall not be sufficient to constitute a divorce. It is constituted only when they divorce and leave each other after a division of the good and bad property in possession and not in possession to which they are entitled

After such a separation if the man or the woman, regarding the other as his former wife or her former husband, has sexual intercourse without the other's consent, he or she shall forfeit all his or her property, and he or she, himself or herself, shall be possessed by the other. If the woman uses obscene language against him, regarding him as her former husband, an indemnity shall be given to the man according to the offence committed.

If there is mutal consent, there is no offence.

S. 172. The man and wife live together and then the man leaves the house, saying " I do not wish to remain, " and as he does not return for long years the wife takes a husband to the knowledge of others ; no damages shall be paid. Should the husband who first left the house again claim her for his wife, and have sexual connection without having sufficient right to claim it, *he* shall be severely punished. If the wife by force does a similar act against the will of her husband, there is right for such a wife to be divorced. If *she* takes a lesser husband, her hair shall be shaved, leaving a cross, and *the man* has a right to sell her ; in other words, after taking away all the property, there is the right for her to be tied and sold either at the bazaar road or other roads. If the husband knowing that his wife has taken a *lesser husband* has again sexual connection with her, he should not charge her with keeping a lesser husband ; let him keep her for his wife as he has done. Thus it has been shown by wise men of old. The words that the man who has had sexual connection with another man's wife should not be killed are shown as testimony in the *Isoola-pa-dco-ma Zat.*

Note.—The above may be compared with ss. 30, 31, and 32 of Bk 6 of the *Menu Kyay.* It may be remarked that the *Wonnana* applies our doctrine of condonation.

Remarks.—The Culāpaduma Jātaka is contained in the Jātaka book of the Sutta pitakam, the second division of the Buddhist canon.

S.173. The husband without the consent of the wife takes another woman ; all debts shall be paid *by him* and he then turned out of the house *naked* as he was born. If either the man or woman endowed with good principles is for a long while suffering from illness, and if the other can no longer resist sexual connection, the man or wife as it may be should ask in kind words leave of the other and then take a new husband or wife as the case may be.

Note —The first sentence enacts a severer rule than our own law. As to this and the last section see the Recorder's judgment in paragraph 13 of my second Note on marriage.

Sections 173 and 132 throw some doubt on the right of polygamy. The present section was not brought to notice in the case where the Special Court affirmed that right (Ma Ing Than's case printed in circular memorandum 8 of the 22nd July 1881). The subject is discussed in paragraph 32 of my second Note, and in paragraph

36 will be found a corrected translation of an important passage in the *Menu Kyay*. In the Special Court I tried to reconcile the ambiguities by holding "that the taking of a lesser wife does not " by itself constitute legal cruelty or give the first wife any addi- " tional rights ; but if he abuses and beats the first, and it be " proved that he has in any way oppressed her, then she may " be entitled to further relief. The section (of the *Menu Kyay*) ap- " pears to mean that there should even be some continuance of the " ill-treatment to justify a resort to the Judges ; and that a passing " quarrel is not enough, but this point is not before us for decision." The Recorder added that polygamy was recognized by the *Menu Kyay* and was established as a custom in British Burma.

S. 174. If a woman buys a man by paying the price of his body and then makes him her husband, and afterwards wishes not to remain, the man is freed from paying the price of the body, but if the man does not love her, he shall not be freed from paying *the price of the body*. If a man pays the price of the body of the woman and then takes her for his wife, and if afterwards the man wishes no longer to live together, the woman is not freed from paying the price of the body ; and if the wife says that she does not wish to remain together nothing is to be said.

Note.—These cases are stated in the same way in the *Menu Kyay*, Bk. 12, s. 36 and other cases of the sort follow.

S. 175. If it is said " leave your husband and live together with me" and the good man's daughter does as is told her by that person, and that man afterwards says "I do no longer want you, " all the property of that good man's son without exception can be taken by that woman. Some wise man say that only what has been exhausted should be taken back. If it is said " leave your wife and live together with me " and the good man's son does as is told him by that woman, should that good man's daughter afterwards say " I do no longer want you, " all her property without exception can be taken by that good man's son. Some wise men say that only what has been exhausted should be returned.

Note.—This section may be described as creating an equity in favour of the man or woman seduced from lawful wedlock into adulterous connection at the expense of the seducer. Unless the seducer remained faithful to the new con- nection he or she had to forfeit the property. In this way the same end might be secured, as the law of England allows by suits for seduction and against the co-re- spondent in a divorce case. I dissent from the reasoning which treats such penal- ties as conferring a tacit approval on breaches of obligations. Their real character seems to be damages, as in the somewhat similar case of a cunning, experienced person entrapping a young person of the other sex into marriage and then aban- doning, for which see sections 57 and 58 of the *Wini Tsaya Paha Thani* translated in para. 41 of my second Note. We see the nature of the process still more clearly in the divorce case described in section 32 of Book 6 of the *Menu Kyay* where the co-respondent is mulcted of his property in favour of the husband and the adulteress not only forfeits hers, but is liable to have her head shaved in four patches and to be sold. See also s 701 of the *Wonnana* and as to sales s. 695. The harlot and the pimp were liable to similar treatment as shown at page 172 of Richardson. The rules of the Hindu law are similar.

S. 176. If a *man is* poor and covered with disease, crippled, foolish, lazy, lustful, old, or, in other words, ignorant, and has certain defects, wives can abuse such a husband, and if through his laziness, madness, and bad conduct he is turned out, *the wife* has that right ; if he accuses, his wife of being a leper, and if the wife says that she does not wish to remain, she h is the right to say so. Learned men should decide that that woman is not entitled to all the property. If the wife abandons her husband because through misfortune he is ill, ugly, and a leper, and does not support him, all should be taken away, and the woman should be punished for three months.

Note.—The Meni Kyιy in Bk. 12, s. 46, states with great fulness the eight causes for which a woman may abuse her husband. Some of them are even to European judgment quite sufficient provocation, and the whole passage must be studied to gain an adequate impression of Burmese sentiment. Then follows this forcible and sensible statement of the doctrine of law (page 358 of Richardson) : " If a woman happen to abuse her husband for any of these eight causes, no fault " shall be imputed to her, and if the husband sue for a divorce, he shall only " obtain it as by mutual consent ; let them divide the property equally and sepa- " ra'e (kwa). There is no law in the world that because a woman is an abusive " wife, her husband shall separate (kwa) and take all the property ; this all " teachers said." Then the wife is enjoined as a religious woman to be submissive, and the beatitude of the hunter's wife is quoted.

The above rules seem to me Hindu as shown by the following texts in Colebrook'e Digest, 57 and 178 : –

Manu.—She who neglects her lord, though addicted to gaming, fond of spiritu-ous liquors or diseased, must be deserted for three months and deprived of her ornamen s and household furniture. But she who is averse from a ma l husband, or a deadly sinner, or an eunuch, or one without manly strength, or one afflicted with such maladies as punish crimes, must neither be deserted nor stripped of her property.

Vasishtha.—From a man of contemptible birth, from an eunuch or the like, from a degraded man, from one afflicted with epilepsy, vicious or tainted with shocking diseases and from a frequenter of harlots, a parent may take back a dam-sel, though given away.

In the section under comment the calling the wife a leper is treated as legal cruelty. Such abuse might in England be actionable slander ; and as I have shown in my second note, the demarking line of legal cruelty varies in the same Court with the advance of opinions. In Burma leprosy is believed to result from sins in previous existences.

Remarks.—The Code of Manu contains a similar passage (V 154) : though (a hus-hand be) unobservant of approved usages, or enamoured of another woman or devoid of good qualities, yet a husband must be revered by a virtuous wife.—Manu IX, 79. But she who is averse from a mad husband, or a deadly sinner, or an eunuch, or one without manly strength, or one afflicted with such maladies as punish crimes, must neither be deserted nor stripped of her property.

Leprosy and other incurable diseases are, according to the *Culakammavibhanga-sutta*, pronounced by Gautama, the result of the following sins : If in this world a woman or man be a tormentor of living beings with the hand, with stones, sticks or knives, upon the d ssolution of his frame by death, he will be born in hell, wretched, miserable and tormented : but if upon dissolution of his frame by death he be not born in hell, but if he again become a man (or woman) wherever he may be born, he will be afflicted with a deadly disease. The path which leads to a state of disease is this : to be a tormentor of living beings with the hand, with stones, with sticks, or with knives.

According to the Vishnu Smriti, leprosy marks a human being who has been a criminal in the highest degree in former existences.

S. 177. If a wife cooks curry and rice well and feeds him and looks after him by giving him betel-leaves and cigars, and also washes and give him his putsoe, &c., and also weaves well and looks after household affairs well, and also looks after *her* son, grandchild, and slaves, and sleeps later than her husband, and eats after her husband, and does nothing without consulting her husband, and listens to what her husband tells her, and is not fond of going from house to house ; if such woman are reviled and struck, and elbowed, that man should be punished (yazadan). It the woman be not as the above, she should in the presence of the elders be severely punished and also be liable to abuse and to be struck. Good wives should look after their husbands, and should they be angry for some cause, injured or suffering from illness, or have any nasty leprosy, as a mother loves her son, as a sister respects her elder brother, as a friend wishes good for a friend, as pupils respect their masters, as servants are afraid and respect their masters, such wives should be well kept by their husbands.

N. te.—Here, as in s. 176, the penal sanction is called in to aid the sanctions of religion and civil law, as in s. 18 of Bk. 5 and s. 30 of Bk. 6 of the *Menu Kyay.* The criminal punishment awardable by elders are of a different sort and severer than the mild chastisements inflicted by the husband in the domestic forum, such. as s. 47 cf Bk. 12 describes. Compare also s. 632 of the *Wonnana,* with s. 701, and as to the resort to tribunals see Note to s. 157 above. They who contend that, in spite of the Burma Courts Act, the loogyees still have a matrimonial and civil jurisdiction will doubtless insist that they still possess the criminal jurisdiction given by the Dhammathat. 1 am of opinion that it ceased with the enactment of the Penal Code and Procedure Code, if not before. The Burman ideas about abuse can be learned from s. 15 of Bk. 9 of the *Menu Kyay.*

S. 178. A good husband who possessing good qualities tries to increase his slaves, property, and household furniture, and builds a good house, and keeps his wife and son comfortably and takes good care of the cattle, and also helps his poor relatives and advises them, should be kept and fed well. If (such care) is not taken, *the woman* shall be severely punished *If the woman* looks after *her husband* and respects and feeds him, the husband should net, abandoning, divorce (mah sun mah kwa) such *a wife.* Persons endowed with these qualities are said to be as *comfortable* as the " Tsat Kya Meng. "

Remarks.—Sakkya Meng, *i.e.,* the King Cakra, is the happy ruler of the Tavattimsa heaven, the lowest devaloka but one, situated on the summit of mount Meru.

APPENDIX A.

Translations of the Chapters on Marriage and Divorce of the Wini Tsaya Paka Thani Dhammathat by Mr. S. Minus and Moung San aided by Moung Kyaw Doon, from the Burmese Text as edited by Moung Tet Too, with Notes by Mr. Jardine and Remarks by Dr. Forchhammer.

ON MARRIAGE.

S. 43. Decisions should thus be given. If a charge is brought thus, "This man has committed adultery with my wife," and if this (charge) is proved, 30 tickels of silver shall be paid, or 300 tickels of copper. If a charge is brought thus, "This woman has committed adultery with my husband," and if this (charge) is proved, the price of the hair-knot and ears should be paid as damage. The price of the hair-knot and ears is 30 viss of copper. If it be an elderly woman and she be a virgin, the fault done is similar to the one done to a virgin. If the charge is denied, evidence to prove the charge should be brought forward ; and if it is proved, the damage should in the same manner be 30 tickels of silver. If not proved, the person who failed to prove shall be the loser. The party who has failed to prove shall pay the expenses of the Court, as also the costs incurred by the other party. If the young couple be of the same position and circumstances in life, let them live together. Thus it should be decided. (*If it is said*) "It is true that sexual connection has taken place, but I do not wish to live together," 300 tickels of copper shall be paid as damage. If made pregnant, 300 tickels of copper shall be paid, which amount is equivalent to 30 tickels of silver, and they both shall pay all the expenses of the Court. If a denial to the effect that it is not true, "I did not not have sexual connection," is made, proof of the charge shall be brought forward. If no witnesses can be shown, let the woman make a correct statement, and if she dare make it, let them live together. If *the man* does not wish to live together, let him pay 300 tickels of copper. If *the woman* say "I do not wish to make a statement." let the man be put under oath, and if he dare do so, the woman who claimed *the man* for her husband shall be the loser. If both of them wish to make correct statements, they should accordingly be chastised or advised. And if even after the advice a refusal to live together be made, the charge should be amended, and in order to clear up *the case, let them* either be made to chew rice or to dive (and see who can remain the longest) and in the diving, the one who *first* appears shall be the loser. (Hear follow some words in Pali, fot the correct translation of which see Dr. Forchhammer's remark on the whole passage). If the loser be the man he shall pay 300 tickels of copper, and if the loser be the woman, she shall pay the expenses of the Court, as also the costs incurred by the other party. If an outsider has connection with a female slave, let him redeem her and live together. If even *he* does not wish to live together, he shall redeem, and set her at liberty. *He* shall neither say that the price of the slave is much nor little, for he knowing the person to be a slave had sexual connection, and should therefore redeem her by paying the original price of *her* body.

Remarks.—The Pāli text is :

Na ahan ti vuttakena, purisena sa tāpaye :
Pi sahe sā parājitā :
Ubho pi satāsiyum, ovādeyya yathārahain :
Ovādakepi nādiye, yathavutta uttanākain :
Tandulam vāpi khadaye, nimāiccaye jale pi vā :
Dakena mujjane pi yo, uttāneva parājito.

If (she) says " Not I, " the man may be put to torment (?) if he persists, she shall be the loser. If both maintain to be in the right, let them be appropriately admonished. If they do not take the correction to heart, let the matter be adjusted as mentioned above, or let them chew rice, or dive under water : he who first frees himself from the water (appears above water) shall be considered as the loser.

S. 44. If it be *with* a woman once married, only 15 tickels of silver *shall be paid.* In some olden books it is said 150 should be paid as damage. This is known to be copper. If *the person* has no silver and copper to pay as damage, the good woman shall take all the property, without exception, *belonging to him.* If it is *done* by a near relative, a slave shall be given. And if the woman does not wish to live, in the same manner damage shall be paid. If it be a lesser wife of another man, 15 tickels of silver, or 150 tickels of copper, shall be *paid.* This alludes to wife, sons, and daughters who are entitled to 30 tickels *of silver.*

S. 45. If sexual connection be had with a young and delicate virgin, 100 *tickels* of copper shall be the damage, or 300 *tickels* of black copper (ေၾက:ဝ:၍) *in olden days meaning lead*, or 30 tickels of pure silver. Either 300 tickels of black copper or 30 tickels of silver. The decision granting the award of 300 tickels of black copper, or 30 tickels of silver (ေၚ), is the only one in accordance *with law.* Decisions should be given after taking into consideration the circumstances and position in life of the suitors.

S. 46. If a person who commits adultery with another man's wife is found and caught in the bedroom, he may be elbowed and struck, and if he even dies there is no damage nor crime ; on the other hand, if the man after leaving the bed arrives near the threshold, there is no right to strike *him.* If *he* is elbowed or struck, *the striker* is liable to pay damage for assault. Damage should also be paid for sexual connection. The relatives have not the right to strike and are not entitled *to get any damage* for the sexual connection. If the act is done in the absence of the husband, *the relatives* should act only according to what they see.

Note by MOUNG TET TOO.

THE decision laid down in olden books in a case of rape on a virgin or a young girl under age as shown in the extract in Pāli is as follows :—
The penalty is 300 tickels of black copper or 30 tickels of pure silver. In another instance, in a case of rape on a virgin or a young girl under age, the penalty is 100 tickels of copper or one viss of silver. I am of opinion that the latter is the proper decision. The penalty

of 300 tickels of black copper or 30 tickels of pure silver is not one for rape, but is mentioned in the Páil extract merely because it is shown in olden books. I concur in what is mentioned in the former, *i.e.*, the penalty of 100 tickels of copper or one viss of silver. In the case of sexual connection or rape, a penalty of 300 tickels of black copper or 300 tickels of pure silver is laid down, but this alludes to a case when *the man* declines to marry after having by mutual consent sexual connection. Therefore I leave the matter for consideration.

S. 47. If *a man* commits adultery with another person's wife, *he* shall pay 30 tickels of silver. If that brutal man again commits adultery with that woman, whose damage has already been paid, *he shall pay* 15 tickels of silver, if he again commits adultery *with that woman, he shall pay* half of what is mentioned above, *i e.*, seven-and-a-half tickels of silver. If he commits it the fourth time, there is no fault. That wicked woman should be numbered amongst the prostitutes. This is mentioned in the *Dkamawelatha* Dhammathat.

In the *Manu* and the *Manutheeka* Dhammathats the above penalties are laid down only when a woman commits adultery with a single individual. In another instance if man commit adultery with *a woman*, the first three men shall each pay damage of 30 tickels *of silver*. If adultery is committed for the fourth time with a separate man, no damage shall be paid. She shall be sold as valued by the Dhammathat and sent to the place of the prostitutes. In the *Manuthaya* Dhammathat it is laid down that such *a woman* is entitled to damage only from two men.

"*Manu*" and "*Manutheeka*" and the "*Manuthaya*" Dhammathats are contradictory on this point; therefore it is left for consideration.

Remarks—The proper spelling of the Páli words is, Dhammavilasa, Manussika and Manusara.

S. 48 In the matter of committing adultery. If either the person who has committed the adultery, or the wicked woman in fault, or the husband who has the right to have sexual connection dies, let there be freedom : consider this. In other words, the penalty for deflowering a virgin varies, as the kinds of virgin differ. The penalty of 30 tickels is said to be *spoken* at random.

S. 49. There are nine kinds of virgins :—

(1) a virgin of the " Min " (ruling class ;
(2) a virgin of the " Poonah " (Brahmin class) ;
(3) a virgin of the trading class ;
(4) a virgin of the cultivating class ;
(5) a virgin of the *same* desires (အခွင့်တူသော) ;
(6) a virgin not of the *same* desires ;
(7) a virgin of the *same* race (သမီးသက်တူသော) ;
(8) a virgin not of the *same* race ;
(9) a slave virgin (ဒါသကတူသော).

These are the nine kinds of virgins. Out of the nine kinds of virgins, if sexual connection be had with the virgin of the ruling class, the damage is 500 ; if with a virgin of the " Poonah " (Brahman class), 400 ; if with a virgin of the trading class, 300 ; if with a virgin of the cultivating class, 200. These are the damages to be paid. If not made pregnant, half of the abovementioned amount only *shall be paid.* Excluding the abovementioned four kinds of virgins, if sexual connection be had with the remaining, a virgin of the same desires, a virgin not of the same desires, a virgin of the same race, and a virgin not of the same race, 300 shall be paid as damage. If not made pregnant, only half of the abovementioned *shall be paid.* If sexual connection be had by force, the whole amount. If either an outside woman who comes under the protection of the parents, or a slave woman, has had connection with her master and gets a child, such a child is called a slave virgin. If sexual connection be had with a slave virgin, two-thirds of the 300 shall be paid as damage. If not made pregnant, only half of that amount. If done forcibly, the whole amount should be paid

---

Note by MOUNG TET TOO.

IN some decisions 500 tickels of pure silver are written by mistake but nothing is known because its origin cannot be traced. My opinion is that if a virgin of the ruling class be taken, 500 tickels of gold is the proper damage, for she is of the ruling family. The 500 tickels of gold at the rate of one viss of silver for every ten tickels of gold amount to 50 viss of silver. Taking this into consideration. I am of opinion that the award is excessive. On the other hand, the price of the Chief Queen is 4,480 tickels of silver only; therefore I am of opinion that the nine virgins are only entitled to tickels of silver, but they may either take gold or silver as they think proper. This is merely the mode of reckoning the amount as is mentioned in the Pali text. Take as suitable.

S. 50. Damages imposed for deflowering virgins is contradictory to what is laid down in the *Manu Thara Shwe Myeen* Dhammathat. Therefore to consider about the different kinds of virgins great intellectual faculty is required. A girl eight years old is called a "gawyee," one ten years old is called a "konemayee," one 12 years old is called a virgin, and one above that *age* is called a "mahaleeki." This is mentioned in several olden books. In other words, on account of her beauty, she is called a virgin. Even if she be 60 years old, if she has never had any sexual connection, *she* must be considered to be a virgin, but, as is mentioned in the book of *Bya Ka Rine*, it is contradictory, and these are merely the words laid down by wise men in the Dhammathats.

*Remarks.—*As is mentioned in the books known as the *Vyakaranas* (see my note on *Bya Ka Rine* under s. 144 of the *Wunnana*).

S. 51. A man without marrying seduces and elopes with a daughter, and if the daughter, after living together and having sexual connection, says that she does not want and does not wish to live with *that man,* the price of the man's body shall be paid, in other words, the price of her body shall be paid to the man. If the man says that he does not like and does not wish to live together, *he* shall pay all the expenses of the suit, and also give up all the property acquired and then get a divorce If both the mother and father, or, in other words, only the mother or only the father, knows and sees and does not speak or prevent, there is no right to give to another man afterwards. Thus it is shown in the *Manu* Dhammathat and **Manutheekha.**

Note by MOUNG TET TOO.

Of the two sentences of the religious book the first is, " If it is " done to the seeing and knowing of both, then only is there the right " to own." The second is " Even if it is done with the knowledge of one, there is the right to own." What is expressed by " Yahzadeetai- mee mahbyatha " is in the *Manu Tsaya* " use discretion."

S. 52. If a person has sexual connection with a virgin against her consent and by force, *he* shall be severely punished and all his property confiscated. If the relations of the offender wish to pay the damage, they can do so by paying 100 tickels of silver. In other words, if sexual connection be had with a virgin against her consent, in the jungle, on the bank of the river, or in a solitary place, let a hundred tickels of pure siiver be paid as damage. If with the *girl's* consent, no damage. If they are of equal position in life, they should marry. If the man declines to live together, he is liable to pay damage : in other words, if sexual connection be had at poays and if the *girl* is made pregnant, let them marry. If *the man* declines, he shall pay 60 tickels as damage and 30 tickels for the child, and in addition to this 30 tickels. If the man is higher in rank and the woman inferior, 30 tickels of *silver* shall be paid as damage if the man does not wish to live together. In other words, if the virgin is pulled about by her hand, let *the man's* left hand be cut off, and if he is afraid to allow this being done, let him pay 60 tickels of pure silver. Even if the virgin consents, a damage of 200 tickels of copper shall be paid. If two virgins rub (*a*) against each other in pleasure, the damage is 200 tickels. If an inferior sends a go-between to one higher in rank, the damage shall be 300 tickels If elderly woman have sexual connection, let the head be shaved and the person turned out of the town. If a man has sexual connection with a woman under the protection of another and makes her pregnant, let *the man* make her his wife. If *he* does not wish to do so, let *him* pay all debts, redeem her and set her, at liberty. These provisions are laid down in the *Manu* Dammathat and the *Meilatha* (*b*). If there be anything remaining, the details of the dignities and rank of the abovementioned will be seen in the *Manu Thara Shwe Myeen Kyan* Dhammathat.

Remarks —(*a*) The Pali text is : *Kinna Kanne* tath' eva ca, *i e.*, (if) virgin with virgin, (let) the same (damage *viz* , 200 tickels, as in the preceding case, be paid). I think it cannot mean anything else than the unchaste conduct of one virgin with another ; the Burmese intrepreter puts the same structure upon it, and the English translation of the Burmese text is correct.

(*b*) Meelatha should be Dhammaweelatha (vilasa), or simply Weelatha (vilasa), is the same book as that noted on page 2.

S. 53. There are eight motives for giving daughters in marriage :—

(1) the belief that *the man* is of high family ;
(2) a promise to make presents in return ;
(3) a promise to do some business or other ;
(4) a promise to relieve from poverty ;
(5) the fact that threats have been spoken ;
(6) a promise to do continuous service ;
(7) a promise to cure a disease ; and
(8) mutual wish.

The daughter is given in marriage because it is believed that *the man* is of high family. If afterwards not of high family as stated, there is a right to take back *the daughter*.

A promise is made that presents will be given in return, and if presents are given as promised, then only *the man* has a right to get *the daughter*. If before the presents are given sexual connection takes place, *the man* has a right to *the daughter* even if the presents shall not be given, *for* the fault lies with the mother and father.

In giving *the daughter* because a promise to do some business is made, three years' service must be done before freedom.

In giving *the daughter* because a promise to perform some important service is made, action towards performance of the promised service should be taken before *the daughter* is given.

If a daughter is given because of threats, there is a right to take her back when the fears subside.

In giving *the daughter* because a promise to do continuous service is made, if sexual connection takes place, that daughter should be that man's wife and no mention should be made about the length of time.

In giving *a daughter* because a promise to cure a disease is made, if the disease is cured, then only *the daughter* should be given to the medical man.

In giving *a daughter* with consent *she* should, according to *her* wish, be given. If the daughter intended dies, one of the remaining daughters should be given, and half of the price of the body of the daughter intended should also be given. Although all the property should have been given, yet, if not given, the price of the body of that daughter or double the presents, or only half of the price of the body of that daughter, should be paid accordingly.

Thus the preceptors of law endowed with the eight duties have pointed out.

ON DIVORCE.

S. 54. The following is the case of divorce(ကွာဆင်း kwa kin) between a husband and wife. If the wife alleges that she is oppressed and ill-treated by her husband by means of harsh language and beating, and if the husband denies the truth of the statement, the wife must prove it. If the evidence shows that the husband was heard abusing and scolding his wife, but was not seen beating and striking her with the elbow, although the evidence does not show that the husband was seen striking his wife, if marks are found on the wife's body, the statement being corroborated by the facts of the marks found on the wife's body, it is to be presumed that the alleged statement of the wife is true inspite of the incompleteness of the evidence given. If the alleged statement is proved, the husband shall bear the costs of the suit, and such husband shall be admonished to live on good terms with his wife, and a written order shall be entered into the effect that the husband will not do the like again on peril of leaving the house with only the dress on his person; nevertheless, inspite of this decision, if the wife claims a divorce because she does not wish to live with him, a divorce may be given as if the consent were mutual. If the husband says "I, too, wish to divorce you," let him be made to leave all the property in the possession of his wife and let them be free. If the husband has no fault and the wife wishes to divorce, let the husband get all the property and such wife shall pay all the debts. If the wife has no fault, the husband shall get the property, and such wife shall pay the incurred debts. If the wife has no fault and the husband wishes to divorce, in this case where the husband divorces it may be decided on the same principle. This is said of a husband and wife married from their younger days.

NOTE.—With the above description of judicial procedure in divorce in the edition of Wonna Kyaw Deng, A.D. 1774, we may compare similar passages in two other books. They are taken from editions printed in Rangoon, and I am unable to say how far the authentic text is preserved.

An abstract of the Buddhist law on divorce as given by Kaingza Manooraza in his "Maharazathatkyee," or Catechism of Law, about A.D. 1640.

1. If a wife proves that her husband has abused, struck, and opposed her although she has not done any fault, the Judge may admonish the husband if this is the first offence. But if the wife persists in saying that she wishes to divorce her husband as he is a severe master to her, and if the husband begs to cohabit with his inexorable wife, whom he promises to regard as his dear life in future, a divorce may be given and their assets and debts should be divided equally between the two. If the husband commits the same offence again, he may be ordered to quit the house with only the dress on his person, leaving all the property with his wife and bearing all the debts incurred by both.

2. If a husband or wife who were married in their younger days (ငယ်လင်၊ ငယ်မယား) wishes to divorce the other without any fault, the party who wishes to divorce shall leave the house with only the dress on his or her person, forfeit all the property to the other, and bear all the debts incurred by both. But if they possess no property at all, let the party who wishes to divorce pay half of the (kobo) price of the body to the other as they are a youthful pair (ngehlin and ngehmaya). A husband and wife are not called ngehlin and ngehmaya when either party has committed adultery, and in virtue of this offence, the offender shall pay the whole of the price of the body to the other and be divorced if the other is concurring.

With Tsaya Paka Thanee of the Nobleman Let Wai Thoondara after A.D. 1774, p. 38.

If a wife who was married when young and who is living in the same house as her husband lodges a complaint in the presence of witnesses with a Judge to the effect that, although she has not committed a half hairbreadth shadow of a fault, she is subjected to the utmost sorrow and misery by her husband using abusive language, slapping, striking her with the elbow, and pulling her hair, and that she cannot account for this strange course of action followed by her husband, and if the husband untruthfully denies committing any of these alleged actions, but admits having admonished and instructed his wife in the discharge of her household duties, and further states that his wife has maliciously made a false charge, the wife shall prove the charge. If the witnesses adduced by the wife depose to the effect that they heard the husband scolding and abusing his wife, and if they do not at all depose as to the husband's beating and striking his wife with the elbow and pulling her about, but if the wife shows marks of beating and striking on her body, it is to be presumed that the wife's statement is circumstantially proved. The expenses for pickled tea, writing fees, and other expenses which had been or would be subsequently incurred, shall be borne by the husband, who may also be subject to a fine. An agreement shall then be entered into between the husband and the wife, by which the former shall bind himself not to abuse or strike his wife in future or ill-treat or oppress her in any other way lest he shall leave the house with the only dress on his pers·n. The parties should also be admonished to live on goodt erms with each other. But if the wife does not consent to enter into such agreement, a divorce may be given as if there is mutual consent. If the wife says that she wants a divorce as her husband caused hurt to her, all the property shall be assigned to the wife and all the debts paid by the husband ; on such condition a divorce may be give. If although the husband is go˄d, the wife inconsiderately insists in getting a divorce, the above law will apply, *mutatis mutandis* to this case. This law applies to husband and wife who were married in their younger days (ngehlin and ngehmaya).

NOTE.—As to the reason and nature of the remedies at Hindu law in disputes or misconduct of husband and wife, see the observations at the beginning of Book 4 of Colebrook's Digest.

S. 55. Misconduct with regard to food is *when a woman* eats before the husband, when she eats with him and goes away before him, and returns without the husband's knowledge and eats with others, or eats often, or buys and eats early, or gives her husband little and eats a great quantity. These are the improprieties in regard to food.

Misconduct towards a man is *when a woman* talks with any man she sees in the same manner as she does with her husband, and laughs, leans, and takes the hand. These are the improprieties towards man.

Misconduct with regard to property is *when a woman* keeps property outside which should be kept inside and keeps property inside which should be kept outside, and without the knowledge of the husband steals, conceals, cheats, sells, buys, gives away, receives, and borrows. These are the improprieties in regard to property.

Misconduct with regard to glances is *when a woman* looks like a crow at other men whom she sees, and winks and turns her eyes in all direction, *when she* opens her clothes and does not cover *herself* properly when bathing, and when she pretends to be asleep. These are the improprieties in regard to glances.

Misconduct with regard to clothes and ornaments is *when a woman* adorns herself without taking into consideration time or place, and when at home or in the jungle, when at ponys (feasts), " mingala " or (funeral gatherings) " ahmingala." These are the improprieties in regard to clothes and ornaments. These are the five kinds of misconduct.

S. 56. The six faults of women are—

(1) *a woman* who is in the habit of drinking liquor ;

(2) *a woman* who goes, comes, and sits with other men ;

(3) *a woman* who is fond of going about to other houses ;

(4. *a woman* who is in the habit of sitting day and night at the doorway ;

(5) *a woman* who does not look after household affairs ;

(6) *a woman* who is in the habit of scolding her husband.

These are the six faults of women which should be known.

Wives who possess any one of these six faults, or of the five kinds of misconduct, should be chastised by striking either with a rope, split bamboo, cane, or a rod (ကြိမ်). If chastisement is not heeded, then only *the wife* may be abandoned or divorced. If elbowed or struck more severely, as it is a fault entitling to a right of divorce *they* should mutually be divorced. Thus it should be decided.

S 57. A divorced man takes a virgin and lives with her, and if after a short time and before much property is acquired, he says to her " leave the house " and divorces her (kwa shin ကွာရှင်း) it amounts to fraud, and for this fault let him compensate her with the value of a pair of " nadoungs " (earrings) : of this it is said that the man is inferior and the woman is superior (in rank). If they are of same class and respectability let him give her the slaves or followers brought at time of marriage, palanquins, sword, the clothes and ornaments worn, and all such things as are brought at such time. Thus it shall be directed. If there are no such slaves or followers, ornaments, elephants, ponies, palanquins and sword, let him give her a slave in his place. If she be thanday-swaikathee (*inciente*) let him give her a slave. If she has already brought forth children let him give her a male and a female slave. The term kowoonshethe (meaning carrying) shall not be used.

S. 58. A divorced woman takes a young man and lives with him, and if she wishes to divorce him without any fault of hers, let her give him the man's clothes and ornaments and turban (or head-dress) and also a slave or follower. If such husband and wife have not acquired much property let them be divorced if they give their mutual consent.

S. 59 If either a woman once married or a young woman takes unto herself her slave for husband, and if afterwards *she* does not wish to live together, she shall forfeit the price of the body and shall give clothing and food and then let the slave husband go.

If either a man once married or a bachelor take unto himself his slave for wife, and if afterwards *he* does not wish to live together, if they have together eaten rice, let the woman accordingly get the (လက်ထက်ပွား) property acquired after marriage, and let the price of the body of the slave woman be forfeited.

NOTE BY MAUNG TET TOO.

On this point in the *Manu Tsaya* it is stated that the original price of the body should not be let off. *My* opinion is that this is proper, if it is required that it should be as that mentioned. The translation of the Pali phrase Dathee-yet-gan-bya-mote-tsa-ya, *(a) meaning* the price of the body of the slave woman should not be let off, should be taken. If even there is no property acquired after marriage, let the price of the body of the slave woman be let off. Otherwise if another wife be taken and if *the man* tells the slave wife that he does not wish to live together, *she* shall not be freed from being a slave If their is desire to be freed, the price of the body shall be paid. Though these points are mentioned in olden books, yet as *the man and the woman* have eaten together, the man has no right to take a new wife. In former decisions there is the right to be divorced, the price of the body to be let off, and the property acquired after marriage to be accordingly given. The latter method is the only one proper. The excellent Minister Manoo Yazar is of the same opinion. Wise men who are acquainted with decisions should consider this.

Remarks (a).—Dasiyaggham pi muccaye (dathee-yet-gan-bya-mote-tsa-ya ?) means the price of the slave woman *should* be let off, even if there be no property of any kind (dhanam asanta kecapi).

APPENDIX B.

IN THE COURT OF THE JUDICIAL COMMISSIONER, BRITISH BURMA.

REFERENCE No. 7 (CIVIL) OF 1876.

Mee Hneen Gnoang *versus* Nga Oung and Mee Lee.

The 11th June 1876.

Circular letter No. 106 of 22nd December 1877. By QUINTON, J. C.—This is a reference under section 25 of the Burma Courts Act.

The opinion of the Court is asked for on this point.—Is the presence of one of the two following conditions necessary in order to constitute a valid divorce between Burman Buddhists, *viz.*, either a decree or order of Court or a written agreement executed by both parties in presence of respectable witnesses specially called together for that purpose ?

The point has not been argued before this Court as no Counsel have been appointed by the parties, and a convenient day could not be agreed upon by two Burman Advocates whom I asked to assist the Court in discussing it

I therefore confine myself to answering the question put. The answer is that the existence of either of the two conditions named is not essential to the validity of a divorce between Burman Buddhists.

2ND APPEAL No. 20 (CIVIL) OF 1876.

Mee Kyeng Maree and others *versus* Mee Htoo Ma.

The 14th September 1876.

Circular letter No. 107 of 22nd December 1877. By QUINTON, J. C.—This suit was brought by a woman against the collateral relations of her deceased husband for property left by him.

The defendants pleaded that the marriage had been dissolved with the consent of the plaintiff prior to the death of the husband, and that therefore the plaintiff had no just claim to share in his estate.

The Court of first instance found that the plaintiff had been a consenting party to a divorce pronounced by the husband, and that therefore the plea of defendants was made out. The Lower Appellate Court considering that the so-called divorce was a " hole-and-corner proceeding " and that it should not be upheld, gave plaintiff a decree. From that decision the present appeal is brought.

I concur with the Deputy Commissioner that plaintiff is entitled to a decree. If there was a valid divorce pronounced, which is open to doubt, I am not satisfied that the wife consented to it. It is admitted by both sides that at the time the so-called divorce paper was written she was out of her mind, and the expression she made use of when the circumstance was reported to her after the recovery of her reason by no means conveys to my mind that she was a willing and consenting party to what had been done ; on the contrary, it amounted to a repudiation of the arrangement as far as it was in the wife's power to repudiate it.

The argument drawn from the conduct of the woman at the funeral is pushed too far. If the woman was really a divorced wife by her own consent, her presence at the bed of the dying man and at the funeral is in itself a most extraordinary circumstance, and the omission of some ceremonial observances by a woman of weak intellect and distracted with grief cannot be used to deprive her of rights to which she would otherwise be entitled.

The deceased died without issue and if, as held by the Lower Appellate Court, there was no divorce, plaintiff is heir to all the property of her husband on the principle of the Burmese law recognized by this Court in the cases of Mee Htoon Bhyoo and others (plaintiffs, Appellants. *versus* Nga Yan, Respondent ; and of Mee Phyoo, Appellant, *versus* Mee Ben Top, Respondent, to be found at pages 29 and 33 of the volume of published rulings.

If, on the other hand, there was a divorce, then, on the finding above stated, the wife was not a consenting party, and she is entitled to all the property acquired since the marriage as well as to what she brought to her.

The law will be found in volume XII of the Dhammathat, page 44 of the new edition I may note here that a negative has been omitted in the sentence at the top of page 344 in the English translation, which completely alters the meaning of the passage.

A portion of the property in suit according to the admission of both parties was acquired after the marriage, being Nos. 1, 2, 3, 4, 5, 6, 8, 9, 10, 12, 13, 14, and 16 of the lots enumerated in the schedule filed, and to this plaintiff's title cannot be contested. Her claim to the remainder hinges altogether on the fact of the divorce. As remarked by the Deputy Commissioner, the so-called divorce was a very " hole-and-corner " proceeding and consisted in the deceased, a short time before his death, sending by her brother to his wife, who was at that time out of her mind, a paper, which has not been produced in the case, but which is allowed to have been an intimation of some sort of the purpose of the writer to divorce the wife. Whether it amounted to a divorce it is impossible to say. The only reason assigned for the wish of deceased to divorce the wife who had lived with him for ten years was that she was mad from grief at the death of her two daughters by a previous marriage. It is perhaps questionable whether a valid divorce can be pronounced when one of the spouses is not in a condition to express dissent or consent in the matter ; and the law as to the treatment of a mad wife is clearly laid down in the 18th section, Chapter V of the Dhammathat in the following passage (page 141 of the old edition) :—

" If the wife be a leper or mad, asthmatic, have her arms or legs broken, is blind, or emaciated and enfeebled, let the husband minister to her in the most proper manner ; he has a right to cease connubial connection with her. He shall have no right to put her away with her property. If he takes a lesser wife, he has a right to do so. If he neglects his first wife and does not take care of her, minister to and support her, one-half of all he possesses be taken and given to her relations ; if he will not give up the property nor support her, let him be punished criminally."

The Lower Appellate Court therefore rightly, in my opinion, refused to give effect to an alleged divorce, the existence of which was very doubtful, and which, if it did exist, is directly opposed to the rule here laid down, a rule altogether in consonance with the dictates of equity and good conscience.

The appeal is dismissed and the decree of Lower Appellate Court in favour of plaintiff upheld with all costs.

MA PPO vs. MOUNG HPO THET.

JUDGMENT.—The plaintiff states that she wishes to be divorced as the defendant (her husband) beats her after taking toddy. The defendant denies having taken toddy and does not wish to be divorced. On taking into consideration their statements, the Court is of opinion that a divorce should not be given for a first quarrel, and as the plaintiff and defendant are youthful man and wife, the Court therefore gives the accused a warning not to drink liquor in future, and directs that they continue to live as man and wife. The defendant to bear the costs

ORDER.—As this is the first quarrel, let them continue to live as man and wife and the defendant pay all costs.

MOUNG HTINE,

The 18th September 1882.   *Sitkeh of Prome .*

MEE OÓ vs. NGA PAN OO.

PLAINT.—Plaintiff, for the undermentioned reasons, wishes to be divorced :—

1. Plaintiff, and defendant were married some seven months ago (both young), and on the 2nd waning of Tawthalin, 1244, corresponding with the 29th August 1882, a dispute arose between plaintiff's mother and the defendant at Mindeh quarter in Thyetmyo, whereupon plaintiff told him that he should not answer back her mother, and for this saying of the plantiff the defendant kept his revenge.

2. That on the 30th day of August 1882 one Mee Hline went and told plaintiff's mother that plaintiff and defendant (man and wife) had a quarrel, whereupon plaintiff's mother, in order to chastise her, said. " if you do not take me to be a human being, don't, even till your death, own me as your mother," and plaintiff unmeaningly said, " I will not stay without owning you as my mother, I would rather be divorced," and so saying went down from the house for a short time, whereupon defendant's mother without any cause abused plaintiff (giving her to her father as wife), and not being able bear it plaintiff in return abused. Defendant's mother then told her son to strike plaintiff, and defendant struck and elbowed plaintiff, for which she prays that a decree granting her divorce may be passed.

5

ANSWER.—Nga Pan Oo, defendant in the above case, humbly begs to state that, for the following reasons, a divorce should not be given :—

1. On the day mentioned in the plaint the plaintiff made use of defendant's turban as a petticoat and therefore defendant told her not to do so, whereupon plaintiff's mother put in her tongue and said "get divorced," Defendant turned round to the plaintiff and told her not to heed her mother's words, but kept no revenge.

2. After this plaintiff's mother came up again and told her daughter in a low tone to get divorced. Defendant then told plaintiff in a low tone not to listen to what her mother told her ; upon this the plaintiff began to abuse (giving defendant's mother to him) and much more, and went to another man's house and there tried to cut her hair with a knife, and the owner of the house was annoyed, and defendant went and begged his pardon and brought plaintiff back to his house.

3. On arrival home defendant told the plaintiff that it was not right for her to have gone to another person's house and there try to cut her hair. In spite of all this the defendant took the bunch of false hair which was in the house and began cutting it, and as the plaintiff was a woman who did not listen to the repeated sayings, defendant struck her with the palm of his hand. Defendant's mother did not tell him to strike his wife. Plaintiff's mother then came up and said that defendant must be divorced, otherwise not to own her for life, and so saying began to drag plaintiff away, and after this only the plaintiff said that she wanted to be divorced.

4. Though an application has been filed asking for a divorce, as defendent is in no way to be blamed, and as he dearly loves the plaintiff, a divorce should not be given.

JUDGMENT.—In accordance with the plaint and the written defence the Court framed issues and examined the witnesses for the plaintiff, who were unable to give corroborative evidence in support of the plaint, and therefore the plaint should not be believed.

ORDER.—The Court does not believe the plaint and therefore dismisses it with costs on the plaintiff.

MOUNG WIKE,
The 13th September 1882.   *Woondauk of Thayetmyo*

MEE AH NAI *vs.* NGA TSIN

SUIT for divorce and for Rs. 139, being the value of property as per list.

JUDGMENT.—In this case the plaintiff stated as follows :—She and the defendant were youthful husband and wife and not being able to pull on got divorced, and after this the defendant took a second wife and then came and asked her for Rs. 25, saying that he wanted to be divorced from his second wife. Accordingly she gave *the amount* ; and as he promised that he would give up all the property if he again took the second wife they again lived as man and wife. They lived together. On the 3rd waxing of Tagoo and on the 15th waxing of the same month the defendant once again took the 2nd wife : there fore, as promised, she wishes a divorce and also to get all the property. The defendant in defence stated that he and the plaintiff by mutual consent got divorce and he received half the property, and since the divorce he has never again taken the plaintiff, and that as the plaintiff had taken away Rs. 30 of his, he asked her for that amount, but only received Rs. 25. That he did not again take the plaintiff and did not promise to give up all the property. Nga Wine, plaintiff's witness, stated that the defendant came and called him to turn a loogyee in the matter of their reunion, that the plaintiff then gave Rs. 25 to be given to the second wife as damages, and that the defendant made a promise that he would give up all the property if he again took the younger wife. Besides this the witnesses produced by the plaintiff and defendant stated that they knew about the reunion, but that they were not there when the reunion took place ; therefore as there is only the evidence of witness Nga Wike, the plaintiff herself was put under oath and examined, and she stated that after being divorced they were again reunited ; that at the time of the divorce the property was divided equally between them ; that there was a promise made at the time of the reunion that if the defendant again took the second wife he would go down the house with only the garments on his person ; that the defendant then brought back all the property taken away when first divorced ; that she had then to give the defendant Rs. 25 to be given to his second wife as damage ; and that, as before stated, the defendant took away the property. The defendant was again examined, and he stated that after he was divorced from the plaintiff they were never again reunited ; that as regards the cow, cart, and bells, they were given to the son temporarily. The Rs. 25, said to be given by the plaintiff, was money not belonging to her, but the plaintiff during the separated period took Rs. 40 of his at Kyoukngeh village, and when he asked back for the money he only received Rs. 10, and that he received Rs. 25 when he said that he wanted to pay Mee Htai as damage and get divorce. and that as for the balance Rs. 5 he did not ask because he was told to give it to the daughter. The plaintiff was again asked before the Court, and she admitted that she received Rs 40 as stated by the defendant, and as it was given for the sons and daughters, the money was accordingly divided amongst them ; and that as regards the cow, bells, and cart, they were left with the son before she and the defendant were reunited. The statement of the plaintiff is similar to that of the defendant. From the beginning they were divorced by mutual consent and the property divided equally, and it has not been proved that at the time of the reunion it was with the plaintiff. Nga Wike, witness produced by the plaintiff, stated that when the defendant took it it was not in plaintiff's possession. and even in the plaintiff's own statement it was shown that before the reunion it was given to the son. As regards the Rs. 25, the plaintiff herself stated, giving the date, that the defendant took that amount. It was by mutual consent that they were divorced. and the plaintiff has stated that the property sued for, which is in defendant's possession, is similar to that in her possession. and as the property in question was by mutual consent divided equally, it is not right to say that the property should be re-obtained. The plaintiff has under oath stated that they were reunited, and the defendant also under oath stated that they were not reunited, and witness Nga Wike stated that he was the person who had to speak about the reunion, and now the Court is of opinion that they should again be divorced and accordingly grants a divorce, and as the defendant is with a second wife, he is directed to pay the plaintiff's costs. The defendant to get the property, valued Rs. 139, which is in his possession.

Moung Loke,
Myo-oke of Kama.

The 18th May 1882.

Dated Rangoon, the 11th November 1882.

2ND CIVIL APPEAL NO. 54 OF 1882.

*Original
Defendants* { 1. MEE SOUNG 2. MEE SA 3. MEE SAN THOO } *vs.* { MEE KOON and MEE PYOO } *Plaintiffs.*

Advocates for Appellants ... GILLBANKS AND SEN.

Ditto for Respondents...VERTANNES.

JUDGMENT.

By JARDINE, J., JUDICIAL COMMISSIONER.—The plaintiffs are sisters of Mee Soung, the 1st defendant. The 2nd defendant is daughter of the 1st defendant, and the 3rd defendant is widow of Moung Paw Hla, who was brother of the plaintiffs and the 1st defendant. Their mother, Mee Too, is still alive and is not a party to this case. The suit was brought for a half share in 62 acres 14 annas and 4 pies of land. The plaint says this land is in possession of 2nd defendant, for which reason she is made a defendant. The ground of claim is stated to be that the land is ancestral and that the plaintiffs are heirs. The plaint further states that in 1877 the mother, Mee Too, without consulting the children, sold 26 acres 7 annas of land to one Nga San Aye for Rs. 110, and that in Civil Case 14 of the 3rd quarter of 1877, in the Court of the Extra Assistant Commissioner of Myema, the present defendants sued Mee Too and San Aye and obtained a decree for the said land on payment of Rs. 110. The plaintiffs offer to pay their share of this amount. The plaint shows no ground for claiming a half in any but the 26 acres 7 annas of land.

Defendant Mee Sa answered that the land had been acquired under the decree of 1877, and since then the defendants had extended the cultivation beyond the 26 acres so received, that plaintiffs knew that Mee Too had first mortgaged and then sold to San Aye, and that they were aware of the facts and did not object.

The other two defendants answered to the same effect, averring that Mee Sa had borne the expenses of the suit of 1877, in which suit the plaintiffs had refused to join, and that they now sued because the land had been improved and the cultivation extended. They urged that the mother, Mee Too, being alive, plaintiffs might sue her, but not them.

The Extra Assistant Commissioner of Myoma found that plaintiffs had declined to join in the suit of 1877, and were precluded by Buddhist law from suing the defendants, as the land had been recovered from the person to whom the mother sold it ; and that as the mother is alive and the children cannot sue for partition until the parents are dead, the present suit will not lie. He further found that the excess over 26 acres was the recent acquisition of the defendants. He dismissed the suit with costs.

The Deputy Commissioner of Toungoo, Major Strover, relying on the texts quoted by Sandford J. in " Nga Myine vs. Mee Baw " (page 39 of Judge Sandford's Rulings), held that a suit for partition may be brought after the parents' death and that the plaintiffs were entitled to a declaration of right. But the decree went further and awarded them half of the land sued for on payment of half of the Rs. 110 and half of the expenses of the suit of 1877. He records that it was admitted that Mee Too owned 62 acres 14 annas and 4 pies of land. This point was, however, contested and made a formal issue in the Original Court and is a ground of appeal here.

The judgment of the Extra Assistant Commissioner of Myoma in the suit of 1877 shows that the present three defendants there sued Mee Too and San Aye for 26 acres and 7 annas. Mee Too said she had sold to San Aye, who said he had bought it from her. The Extra Assistant Commissioner treated this sale as a mere mortgage and his judgment contains the following assertions—" The land belongs " to Mee Too : on her death the present three defendants inherit. Im- " moveable property cannot be sold without the consent of the chil- " dren (vide pp. 181 and 43 of the Menu Kyay Dhammathat). The " children may mortgage it for charitable purposes. If it were neces- " sary to sell the land for necessary subsistence, the mother must, " before selling to a stranger' give the daughters an option of buying " it."

The issues requiring distinct findings appear to me to be the following :—

(1).—Did the plaintiffs refuse to join the defendants in bringing the suit of 1877 ?
(2).—If so, are the plaintiffs thereby estopped from bringing the present suit ?
(3).—Have the plaintiffs proved that the part of the 62 acres 14 annas 4 pies in excess of the 26 acres 7 annas awarded in 1877 belonged to Mee Too ?
(4).—Have the plaintiffs proved any right to any land except the 26 acres 7 annas ?
(5).—Are daughters entitled to sue for a share of the property of their parents on the death of the father or must they wait till the mother is dead also ?
(6).—Are plaintiffs entitled to any relief in the present suit, and, if so, to what relief ?

On the 1st issue, I am of opinion that the plaintiffs did in 1877 decline to join in the suit brought by the three defendants to recover the 26 acres 7 annas from San Aye. The witnesses of both sides say so : the plaintiffs said they did not wish to sue, the reason being apparently that they did not wish to sue their mother. On the 3rd and 4th issues, I find that plaintiffs have not proved that any land in excess of 26 acres 7 annas belonged to Mee Too or was ancestral, and that plaintiffs have not proved any right whatever to any land in excess of that quantity. Defendants being in possession, it was for the plaintiffs to prove any rights they possess ; but they did not even aver such rights in their plaint, and when on defendants' denial a distinct issue was raised, they produced no evidence except the very vaguest. Defendants have produced more circumstantial evidence to show that the excess over the 26 acres 7 annas is their own acquisition since the decree of 1877. I believe this evidence and find against plaintiffs and for defendants as regards the excess. I concur with the original Court and the opinion of the assessor Moung Shway Waing, the other assessor having given no opinion.

On the second issue my opinion is that there was nothing in the circumstances of plaintiffs' refusal to join in the suit of 1877 which would at Buddhist law or in equity preclude them from suing now. The evidence does not convince me that they gave up to defendants without consideration such rights as plaintiffs possessed in the land They merely refused to join in that suit. If estopped at all, it is by limitation ; and in the present appeal I need not consider that point. If at Buddhist law the widow had a right to make an absolute sale, the plaintiffs cannot bring this suit. If she had a life-interest only, neither she nor the defendants who have recovered the land from her vendee can be sued during her lifetime. as it is not said that she is imbecile, as there is no contention that the widow forfeits at Buddhist law her rights when she makes an illegal sale, and as there is no question raised in this case about the eldest son or the eldest daughter not having on the death of the father received the share to which he or she was entitled when that event occurred. I note this last fact to distinguish the present case from that of Nga Shway Yoh vs. Mee Tsan Byoo printed in circular memorandum No. 22 of the 3rd October 1881. The judgment there perhaps conveys the impression that any of the children has an immediate right to sue on the death of either parent. But the opinion of the assessor, Moung Bah Wah, in that appeal was based on the fact of the eldest child having a right at Buddhist law to demand a share which, he assumed, had not been given him before the sale by the widow ; and in the argument, the question of the particular kind of relief to be given was not discussed whether as claimed by recovery of the land or, as might have been argued, by a fresh suit for a declatory decree under the 43rd section of the Specific Relief Act. The point really decided by that judgment was that, without some family necessity. the widow could not effect an absolute sale of property which she and her husband had jointly acquired, unless the children gave consent to such sale It was on this broad question that the assessors, Moung Ohn and Moung Bah Wah, differed.

In the present appeal Moung Kyaw Doon's opinion seems to be really that the land was wrongly recovered from San Aye, and must now be treated as forming part of the undivided inheritance in which the daughters of Mee Too have rights. But at the same time he is of opinion that the daughters cannot claim a division from the mother, and I fail to see how any but a declaratory suit can be brought during Mee Too's lifetime. The cases of Nga Myine and of Mee Tai, decided by Sandford J. and printed at pages 37 and 40 of his Rulings, are quite different from the present ; and those careful judgment, though valuable aids to consideration of the spirit of the Buddhist law, seem to me not otherwise in point.

On the fifth issue my finding is that younger daughters are not entitled to sue the mother for a share of the property on the death of the father, but must wait until the mother is dead also before they can claim their shares.

In dealing with this question, I have been led to consider what the Buddhist law ordains as to the status of the children before the father dies, so that its general spirit shall not be ignored in deciding this particular point. As Sandford J.'s rulings show, the present possessor of property has sometimes large powers of sale and yet the relations of the seller may insist on pre-emption from the purchaser in case the latter wishes to sell again. The 10th Book of the *Menu Kyay* carefully secures the children's share of property against a step-parent in certain cases, and yet leaves large powers over the residue : and it is not easy at once to say under such a law when the right of bringing suit arises. On this fifth issue, which is of general importance to the Buddhist community, no decision of either this Court or the Recorder's Court has been shown me either on the interpretation of the written law or on the custom of the people. In Nga Shway Yoh's case the assessors held different opinions : Moung Ohn, a former Judge of the Small Cause Court at Rangoon, holding that the widow had the right to make an absolute sale and that the law which invalidates the sale of ancestral property and which Sandford J.'s decisions declare, is inapplicable to the case. Moung Ohn held that the widow had as much power of absolute sale as she and her husband had jointly possessed during the husband's lifetime ; and seems to have held that she became absolute owner of all but the portion of the eldest son or the eldest daughter and could dispose of all but such portion as she chose, irrespective of family necessity or the interests of the children, and that the purchaser got by such sale a valid title so as to preclude the children, whether they had consented or not, from ever contesting the vendee's rights.

In the present appeal the counsel agreed that it was vain to expect any clear evidence about established custom ; and as no issue about custom was demanded, and as in Nga Shway Yoh's case I had ascertained from different Native Judges that they had never personally known of cases of out-and-out sales by widows without consent of the heirs, I thought it unnecessary to frame any issue on which evidence of custom should be taken. In the absence of decisions, of translations of any Dhammathats except the *Menu Kyay,* and on consideration of the obscurity of the Burmese phraseology, I was averse to deciding a doubtful question of the law of inheritance without Native assistance, and I accordingly selected as assessors in the present appeal Moung Kyaw Doon and Moung Shway Waing. The former was for years an Extra Assistant Commissioner and has made a study of the Dhammathats, the latter is an Extra Assistant Commissioner. Moung Shway Waing agrees with Moung Kyaw Doon in holding that the children other than the eldest son or eldest daughter may not demand their shares of the inheritance until both parents are dead. But he appears to me to hold that the widow's power of absolute sale is limited to circumstances of family necessity, and that she only takes a life interest in the residue of the property and that her children on her death may demand the property sold to the purchaser. The Extra Assistant

Commissioner of Myoma in the suit of 1877 was of different opinion as he reversed the sale of the land by the widow during the widow's lifetime. Where Burmese Judges differ so much in their intepretation of the written law, it is not easy for me to give judgment without feeling the danger of mistake occuring. I notice the fact that both the present assessors say that widows very seldom sell the inheritance where no family necessity exists, unless the children first consent, without a remonstrance from the children if they are old enough to remonstrate. Two instances of successful remonstrance, namely, the case of 1877 and Shway Yoh's case, are on record. These facts must be remembered in an inquiry into the general spirit of the Buddhist law as it would be unsafe to ignore that in the construction of one or two doubtful sentences relating to a particular point. In interpreting Buddhist law there is greater difficulty than at Hindu law because the Buddhist civil law of inheritance is not so closely connected with religious ideas. In some places the connection is more visible than in others, but we have at present no means of determining the relative age of different parts of the Dhammathats.

In several places the children are treated as owned by the parents, and this doctrine pervades much of the law of marriage, e.g., Bk. 6. ss 21 and 23 of the *Menu Kyay*. It is also stated in s. 80 of Bk. 10. In Bk. 3 the sale of children is allowed, and elsewhere the division of children between the parents on divorce is provided for. The 30th section of the 6th Book punishes desertion of parents ; and in Bk. 12, s. 47 the doctrine is laid down that an utterly incorrigible child may be driven away and disinherited. The first assumption is, I think, that parents and children live together ; the children may marry with consent of parents, and with this consent or acquiescence a sort of emancipation may be made by a grown-up son or daughter taking some of the property and setting up a separate establishment (Bk. 10, ss. 22 to 24, 29 to 32). In Bk. 3, ss. 33 to 37, the separation and division during the parents' lifetime is mentioned : the children living separate are compared to fruit and blossom which have fallen from the tree. In Mee Phyoo's case (Sandford's Rulings, p. 33) the application to the state of things of the law laid down in s. 30 of Bk. 6 will be found. The parent sometimes after the children had separated went to live with a son or daughter, and a child sometimes returned to the parental house. All these circumstances admit of natural explanations. I adduce them to avoid expressing a general proposition without the right limitations. There can be no doubt that living together is a great fact in Buddhist law, and that the children are to be subordinate to the parents until they obtain a more or less independent position.

But the position of the eldest son, the Auratha or Thagyee as he is called, is superior to that of the others. In the list of children in s. 81 of Bk. 10 it is said that the Auratha only has a perfect right to the property of his parents. Other children cannot demand property from the surviving parent on the ground that the deceased parent had promised it. In the division under s. 50 the Auratha has the first choice. At ss. 15, 22, and elsewhere it is said he takes the father's place : this may be when the father is dead or when both parents are dead. He is superseded if deaf or blind by a younger brother under s. 36 ; and possibly s. 35 imposes on the Auratha the burden of maintaining a brother helpless from disease. He has a duty to perform, but whether this duty is a mere moral obligation or can be enforced at law is at present undetermined so far as decisions go. The *Manoo Wonnana*, s. 10, and the *Manoo Shwe Myeen*, s. 12, describe this duty as the taking up of the father's burden or responsibility; and it is when this burden is assumed that the eldest son is to get the elephant, horse, sword, goblet, betel-box, and other articles used by his father. Under certain circumstances the eldest daughter, at least when there is no son competent to assume the parental duty, takes the paraphernalia of the deceased mother, as at s. 3 of Bk. 10 of the *Menu Kyay*, where she takes her mother's ornaments, clothes, and the slaves who cooked her rice. These rights to paraphernalia, though expressly stated in the three Dahmmathats above quoted, are not even mentioned in Sparks' Code. They are rights additional to the fractional share of the inheritance which on the death of one parent the eldest son or eldest daughter is entitled to demand from the surviving parent.

During the life of the parents the children have some rights of user, at least while they live with the parents, but without the parent's consent they cannot waste or give away the property (see Bk. 6, s. 43. and Bk. 8. s. 3. about gifts). The wife and the scholar are placed under the same restrictions. But at page 239 of Richardson's *Menu Kyay* occurs a passage which shows how closely the Buddhist law fits with the ordinary circumstances of life : how the same necessity created the same equitable doctrine in England and Burma : how careful a foreign Judge should be in stating exceptions whenever he deals with a general rule laid down for the first time. If the parents have become silly from old age, and without the children's consent give away the property, the receiver must give it back if the children demand it. A definite and reasonable ruling like this seems to me to throw great doubt on the rigid rule stated on the Bench by Moung Kyaw Doon, namely, that the surviving parent may if she pleases sell the land and throw the price into the sea and that the heirs have no right to object. The more I study the Buddhist law the more it seems to me to accord with the life of the people and the usual facts : and I incline to think it important in interpretation to give the same recognition to moral duty and to equitable doctrines as is given by the Dhammathats. Otherwise we shall divorce law from morality and equity and be forced to such conclusions as the absurdity above stated. The notion of the Buddhist law is that the family lives together and that the children are subordinate to the parents. The rule of the road given at s. 22 of Bk. 7 has a general reason : a scholar must yield to his teacher : children to their parents : the young brother to the elder : one with a light burden to one with a heavy one. But as we have seen the parents often let the children set up separate houses : and the aged parent or grand-parent some times wishes to spend the closing years of life under the guardianship of a child So that the general rules of subordination cease to apply where all the circumstances have changed.

Having now considered how the children stood in relation to parents and to each other we can consider whether there is reason to suppose that any child can on the death of the father demand a share of the inheritance from the surviving mother. The subordination is due to parents, the word being plural.

The 68th section of Sparks' Code gives some apparent sanction for such claims. It is as follows :—"In the division of an estate between

" the surviving husband or wife and children, the widow or widower
" shall take the dwelling-house and three-fourths of the estate, and the
" children divide the remaining one-fourth equally among them."

The two assessors are distinctly of opinion that this is bad law : they say they never heard of the younger children sharing in the one quarter share given to the eldest son or of this share being chargeable with the maintenance of the younger children. They say that where the Dhammathat awards an eldest son a quarter share he takes it absolutely and is not entitled afterwards to share with the other brothers and sisters in the other three quarters on the death of the surviving parent. The only text to support Major Sparks' view quoted in this argument is s. 2 of Kyaw Deng's edition of the *Wini Tsaya Paka Thani*, of which the translation is as follows :—

" 2. After the death of the father (the inheritance) shall be divided between the mother and sons in the following manner. The mother to take all the female slaves, and the things used by the father, such as his riding horse, sword, etc., shall be given only to the son. After thus dividing the remaining property shall be divided into four equal parts and one-fourth given to the son and three-fourths to the mother. It there are sons of the same parents, the one-fourth shall be divided between them in the following manner:—The said quarter shall be divided into 10 parts and two-tenths shall be given to the eldest son. The balance shall then be again divided into 10 parts and the elder son shall get $1\frac{1}{2}$ parts : the balance shall then be again divided into 10 parts and one part given to the son next to the second. The balance shall then be again divided into 10 parts and half of one part given to the youngest son ; and the balance after such division shall be equally divided among all the brothers. Thus in this manner division (of property) shall be made among children of the same parents."

I have already mentioned that in Shway Yoh's case the assessor, Moung Bah Wah , took the view expressed by Major Sparks. But it does not appear distinctly stated anywhere in the *Menu Kyay*. In s. 5 of Bk. 10 the rule of division between the mother and sons on the death of the father is thus stated :—"Let the residue be " divided into four parts, of which let the eldest son have one, and the " younger daughters with the mother have three." So in s. 3, where the father and daughter divide on the death of the mother, it is said : " Let the residue be divided into four shares, let the daughter have one and the father three." It is difficult to understand why the maintenance of the younger children should, when the surviving parent does not marry again, be transferred from that parent who keeps the bulk of the property and be imposed on the eldest son or eldest daughter. In the *Wonnana*, s. 10, the rule of division between mother and sons makes no mention of younger children ; the mother gets three shares and the eldest son one share. It is the same in s. 12 of the *Shwe Myeen*. It is not necessary to go further into the law on this subject as the suit is not brought for a share in the *peculium* of the eldest child. I have had to consider it because, if the law was correctly stated by Moung Bah Wah, and if the younger children are entitled to share in that portion, the suit should have been brought for partition of the share of the eldest child and not for a half share of the estate during the mother's lifetime. We have tried to put some reasonable meaning on ss. 11 and 12 of Bk. 10 of Richardson's

Menu Kyay about partition of a fourth share among relations on the death of the surviving parent, but without success. It is, however, unnecessary to deal with these sections as the mother is still alive.

In s. 13 the rule is laid down for partition when both parents are dead, leaving only daughters, and in s. 14 when only sons are left, and when both sons and daughters are left. But no rule has been shown, either in the *Menu Kyay* or any other Dhammathat, allowing any but an eldest son or eldest daughter to claim a share until both parents are dead. The *Menu Kyay*, as already noticed, awards three-quarters to the mother with the younger daughters on the death of the father: the other Dhammathats quoted do not mention the younger daughters. Any ambignity that remains appears cleared up by s. 9 of the *Wonnana* and s. 25 of the *Shwe Myeen*, which expressly mention the death of both parents as precedent to the general rights to claim a share in the inheritance. I note that the words translated by Dr. Richardson as *parents* usually mean *father and mother* in the Burmese language, and very often the words *two persons* are found in the Burmese text.

On the sixth issue, I am of opinion that the plaintiffs are not entitled to any relief in this suit. There is no claim as eldest daughter. The mother has not been made a party. There is no prayer for a declaratory decree. There is nothing to my knowledge in the circumstances of the case to entitle to other relief at Buddhist law in the present suit. It is thus unnecessary to discuss further whether the widow takes a life-interest with a power of sale only in case of necessitous circumstances or otherwise. On this point the assessors differ and the *Wonnana*, in s. 11, gives greater power to waste the property to a widow who marries again than is given by the *Menu Kyay*, which looks on second marriages as common and on step-parents with a natural jealousy.

I append to this judgment the opinions of the two assessors and their statements to the Court, and translation of the following texts:—

Manoo Wonnana, ss. 9, 10, 11, and 17; *Manoo Shwe Myeen*, ss. 12 and 25.

There is less difference of opinion on the fifth issue than might have been expected, and fewer differences in the texts than might have been looked for, when we remember that, until 1848, the law was only to be found on palm-leaf manuscripts, and had to be interpreted without the aid of earlier judicial decisions. Possibly the reason why none can be found is that the proposition is too clear and the law too well known. In fact Mr. Vertannes has not seriously contested Mr. Gillbanks' argument that the general partition cannot be claimed until both the parents are dead.

I now reverse the Deputy Commissioner's decree and restore the original decree, the respondents to pay costs of both appeals.

The opinion of Assessor MOUNG KYAW DOON.

IN this suit, one Mee Soung, together with her daughter, Mee Sa, and her brother's wife, Mee San Thoo, sues her mother, Mee Too, and Nga San Aye, the buyer of the land in dispute, to redeem the said lan l, which the plaintiffs allege was sold without their knowledge or permission to the said Nga San Aye, who is a stranger. On weighing the whole of the matters of fact contained in the plaint, the written statements, and the evidence given for both sides, I find that the plaintiffs have no right to redeem the land in dispute. This opinion is grounded on the following points of law :—*Menu Kyay Dhammathat*, Bk. 10, s. 4, says that on the death of the father the mother shall give one pay of paddy land and a share of the cattle to her daughter. But *Manoo Wonnana*, s. 11, and other Dhammathats amended this clause about land, and distinctly say that the mother has a right to dispose of not only the said pay of land, but also the whole of the property. The land in question is not to be deemed ancestral property as the defendant, Mee Too, who is the mother, is still living, and until her death it cannot be regarded as such.

2. In support of my opinion another quotation my be made :— *Wini Tsaya Paka Thani*, which is in universal use among the Judges, Khones (Cadies), Advocates, etc., of Burma, says :—"The daughter has " a right to keep in her possession such property given to her during " the lifetime of her father and mother as dowry, gold earings, gold " necklace, bodkins, etc." As this section does not contemplate the giving and receiving of any land, I do not hold that the plaintiffs, Mee Soung, Mee Sa, and Mee San Thoo, have a legal right to claim the land now in dispute. The plaintiffs cannot claim and receive any land unless it was positively given them by their father during his lifetime.

3. The *Manoo Wonnana* Dhammathat, *Wini Tsaya* Dhammathat, and Bounggyoke palm-leaf manuscript Dhammathat collection of Burmese law, which are generally referred to by the Burmese Judges and Khones, go to show that the daughter has a legal right to keep in possession such property as was given her in the presence of the mother by her father during his lifetime.

There is not one passage in the above cited Dhammathat showing that the daughter is legally entitled to the remaining property in her mother's possession Therefore the plaintiffs have no right to claim the land now in dispute.

4. The defendant, Mee Too, had a son called Nga Paw La. This Nga Paw La, after his marriage and before he died, never did take possession of any portion of the land in dispute and work it, although he had a right to claim and receive one-fourth of it from his mother. And as this son died leaving no children who could claim his inheritance, the land in question should be left in Mee Too's possession.

5. After the decision of this case Mee Koon and Mee Phyoo brought a suit against the said Mee Soung, Mee Sa, and Mee San Thoo, claiming to be admitted into the possession of the land in dispute after giving their share of money, as the parties are sisters and co-heirs. With reference to this point at issue, various Dhammathats state that as there are seven kinds of ancestral property and as the defendants, who are co-heirs, have been keeping the land in question in their possession and enjoying its produce, the ancestral land should not be divided, but the parties according to their priority of birth, i.e., eldest, elder, younger children, should be admitted into the possession of the land now in dispute.

The opinion of MOUNG SHWAY WAING, Extra Assistant Commissioner.

THE principal points which require to be considered here in this case are :—

    1st.—Whether an inheritance can be divided in the lifetime of one of the parents.

    2nd.—Whether a surviving parent has a right to sell the whole or portion of such undivided inheritance without the knowledge or consent of the children.

    3rd.—When the inheritance which has been absolutely sold by the surviving parent, being redeemed by some of its heirs, could the other children, who did not join in recovering such property, claim for shares.

According to the Buddhist law and to the general custom, the partition of inheritance cannot be made in the lifetime of surviving parents (Chap. 1, s 25, of *Manoo Thara* (Shwe Myeen), and vol. 10, s. 11 of *Menu Kyay*.

Under ss. 4 and 5, vol. 10 of *Menu Kyay*, and ss. 12 and 13 of *Manoo Thara*, an eldest son or an eldest daughter on the death of the father is entitled to his or her share of certain property, such as an elephant, horse, slave, etc., and the mother and younger children take all the residue of the property, animate and inanimate. But if the eldest child be a son and demands one-fourth of such residue, it will go to him and three-fourths to the mother and younger children.

The younger children have no right over such residue during the lifetime of the surviving parents, who can sell the whole or a portion of such property for necessary subsistence (vol. 10, ss. 4 and 5 of *Menu Kyay*). But as a general custom such property should only be sold to a stranger when other heirs to the property are not willing to accept the bargain.

When property is sold to a stranger by a surviving parent and is afterwards redeemed by some of the heirs, they hold the said property as purchasers by pre-emption and not as sharers ; therefore the other heirs who did not join or contribute anything towards its redemption can claim no shares in that property.

In this case it appears that Mee Kwon and Mee Pyoo first instituted a suit in the Myo-oke's court at Toungoo against Mee Soung and two others to recover 31 acres 7 annas 1 pie of land valued at Rs. 300 as their share of inheritance.

The Myo-oke after enquiry dismissed their claim on the grounds that their mother is still living and the land in question is one redeemed by means of an action after it had been absolutely sold by their mother. But this decision was reversed in appeal by the District Court of Toungoo, and it decreed that the appellants were entitled to 31 acres 7 annas 1 pie of the land in question on payment of Rs. 55 and half the expenses of the suit in which respondents redeemed the land from one San Aye.

It was alleged that the land originally sold to San Aye by their mother was only 26 acres, which increased to an extent of 62 acres 14 annas and 4 pies in five years' time, after it had been recovered from the possession of San Aye by gradual extension of cultivation on adjoining waste lands. I am therefore of opinion that the actual increment of land brought under cultivation by respondents, *viz.,*

36 acres 14 annas and 4 pies should not be taken as ancestral property, and the original land which has been redeemed by them from San Aye should be treated as their own private property, upon which their other sisters have no claim for shares.

Statements of Assessors MOUNG KYAW DOON and MOUNG SHWAY WAING to the Court.

THEY admit that the principal difference of opinion is this :— Moung Kyaw Doon considers the plaintiffs to be entitled now to share with defendants as co-sharers, whereas Moung Shway Waing is of opinion that this relationship does not exist, but that defendants have by pre-emption got a different right of their own, and that plaintiffs are not entitled to share either now or on the death of the mother, Mee Too, as they acquiesced in her sale.

Moung Kyaw Doon says he refers to *Manoo Wonana* (ss. 10 and 11), *Manu Kyay* (Bk. 10, s. 4), and *Wini Tsaya Paka Thani* (Let Wai Thoondara's edition).

Both assessors say that an eldest son on his father's death is entitled, over and above the elephant, horse, and other things used by his father, to one-fourth of the residue at once and without waiting for the mother's death. But that an eldest daughter is not entitled to this fourth. Both say also that he takes this one-fourth without liability to maintain the other children or to share it with them. Both say that the eldest son who has received one-fourth is not entitled to share in the other three-fourths on the mother's death. Both say it is the mother's duty to maintain the other children out of the three-fourths so long as they are under her control. Both agree that the widow may sell without any necessity at all, but as to whether the sons and daughters, even if they did not consent to the sale, can or cannot at her death demand to redeem the land or demand to purchase in preference to a third person, to whom the widow's vendee is about to sell, they differ in opinion. Moung Kyaw Doon saying that the children have no such powers, and Moung Shway Waing that they have. Moung Kyaw Doon says that at time of sale there is a distinction between permanent and temporary sale (poungthay and poungshin). Both state that they have very seldom known of a widow with children old enough to remonstrate selling the three-fourth share without necessity without a remonstrance being made. Both agree that s 68 of Sparks is all wrong and never heard of ; the young children, they say, must be cared for by the mother although it is so laid down in s. 2 of Let Wai Thoondara's *Paka Thani*).

[TRANSLATIONS.]

Manoo Wonnana Dhammathat edited by MOUNG TET TOO.

S. 9. If there be many slaves and property which should be called inheritance, they shall not be divided during the lifetime of the father and mother, i e., two individuals.

S. 10. There are seven ways of demanding inheritance from the father and mother as mentioned in the beginning, and of these seven ways the following shall be considered as the rule of inheritance between the mother and sons : After the father's death, if the son bears the father's responsibility, such eldest son gets the lance used by the father, and also all such articles of use, and elephant, betel-box, teapot, cups used in betel-boxes, sword-bearer, umbrella-holder and other followers, being animate and inanimate things always used (by the father). He shall also, in the first instance, get the riding horse and ass and also the vegetable garden, paddy land house, and land separately. No son shall forcibly take the waistband, earrings, hairpin, bracelets, ring. etc., palanquin, cymbals, as are given to wear and use during the father's lifetime. Of the bullocks, buffaloes, goats, pigs and paddy land, being property other than those described above, the mother shall get three shares and the son one share. Besides these remaining inanimate property, *viz*, gold and silver, shall be divided in the same manner The son was unable to give any assistance at the time the property was acquired ; and the father did not take care of the property that was acquired, and for this reason the mother is entitled to get three shares, and if the son takes his father's place he gets one share. As the mother had been looking after and feeding them she shall get three of the male slaves and the son one. The mother shall get all the female slaves. Even if there be 10 sons, it shall be the same. If there be female slaves only, the mother shall divide them and give an appropriate number to the son. This relates only to ' letthatpwa " property and slaves. If there be any slaves brought by the father, they shall be divided equally with the mother. The division between the daughter and father as far as it relates to slaves shall be the same as this.

S. 11 Bracelets, rings, earrings. necklaces, given to the daughter by her parents during the lifetime of the father shall be given to the daughter alone. The family of slaves, cows, and buffaloes by pairs shall also be divided. Indian-corn, peas, and paddy shall be given to the daughter as much as she deserves, and the balance to the mother. If the daughter be married and lives in a separate house, she alone is entitled to all things given her by her parents at the time of her marriage. If the daughter be one who eats and lives together with her parents, though she be from a respectable family, the mother being with her, has the control over all the property. The mother of such daughter can make use of the property, can feed a second husband, and can make offerings, and even if the whole property become exhausted she cannot be blamed. If asked why the girl who is from a respectable family should not get any property by her being together with her parent, the reply is that the mother has control over her daughter. If the mother during her lifetime makes use of all the property and the property becomes exhausted, let it be so, but if any property be left, the daughter alone takes possession of the said property. Therefore she who lives with her parent has to remain without anything before.

S. 17. The following is the way of dividing the ancestral property among the children born of the same parents, after their (mi-pa) parents' death :—The eldest son shall receive two shares, the elder one-and-a-half shares, the youngest one share. The shares of the eldest, elder and youngest daughters shall be in the same proportion as those of the eldest, elder, and youngest son. The eldest son and the eldest daughter shall receive their share of cattle in the same propor-tion. This law of division applies to unmarried children.

Manoo Thara Shwe Myeen Dhammathat edited by MOUNG TET TOO.

S. 12. Of these seven kinds the following is the division (of inheritance) between mother and son on the death of the father : If the son happens to bear the father's responsibility, such son shall first get the lance used by his father and also the elephant (always used by his father), likewise horse, the slave who carries the betel-box, paddy land, house, and plantation, as also a putsoe and a jacket. The mother shall get three-fourths of cows, buffaloes, goats, Burmese goats, native fowls, pigs, and such like, and the son one-fourth. No son shall forcibly take the waistband, earrings, bracelets, anklets, cymbals, palanquin, as are given to wear and used during the lifetime of the father. Of the gold, silver, copper, iron, paddy, Indian-corn, gram, cotton, and sessamum-seeds, etc., being other than those described above, the mother shall get three shares and the son one share. The son was not born at the time the property was acquired, and the father was unable to give any assistance in looking after the said property, and therefore the mother is entitled to get three shares, and as the son takes his father's place he gets one share. As the mother had been looking after and feeding them she shall get three of the male slaves, and the son one. The mother alone is entitled to get the female slaves, and not the son. Even if there be 10 sons, it shall be the same.

S. 25. If the father and mother are alive and not dead, the sons and daughters shall not enjoy the inheritance. Such sons and daughters shall get and enjoy the inheritance only on the death of the father and mother.

www.ingramcontent.com/pod-product-compliance
Lightning Source LLC
Chambersburg PA
CBHW081221020426
42331CB00012B/3065